His dream an emblem to us of the life of thought,
The same dream that then flared before intelligence
When light first went forth looking for the eye.
                    HOWARD NEMEROV

Splintered Light

Logos and Language in Tolkien's World

by

VERLYN FLIEGER

Wm. B. Eerdmans Publishing Company
Grand Rapids, Michigan

| *This book is for my students* |

Copyright © 1983 by William B. Eerdmans Publishing Co.
255 Jefferson Ave. S.E., Grand Rapids, Michigan 49503
All rights reserved
Printed in the United States of America

Library of Congress Cataloging in Publication Data

Flieger, Verlyn, 1933-
Splintered light.

1. Tolkien, J. R. R. (John Ronald Reuel), 1892-1973.
Silmarillion. 2. Light and darkness in literature.
3. Christianity in literature. I. Title
PR6039.032S5325 1983   828'.91209   83-14204
ISBN 0-8028-1955-9

We gratefully acknowledge permission to reprint portions of Chapters III and IV, which first appeared as "Barfield's *Poetic Diction* and Splintered Light" in *Studies in the Literary Imagination,* Vol. XIV, No. 2 (Fall 1981).

Grateful acknowledgment is also given to the Houghton Mifflin Company for permission reprint excerpts from the following works:

The Letters of J.R.R. Tolkien by Humphrey Carpenter. Copyright © 1981 by George Allen & Unwin (Publishers) Ltd.

The Lord of the Rings by J.R.R. Tolkien. Copyright © 1965 by J.R.R. Tolkien.

The Silmarillion by J.R.R. Tolkien. Copyright © 1977 by George Allen & Unwin (Publishers) Ltd.

Tolkien: A Biography by Humphrey Carpenter.

The Tolkien Reader by J.R.R. Tolkien. Copyright © 1966 by J.R.R. Tolkien.

| CONTENTS

| ACKNOWLEDGMENTS

I would like to begin by acknowledging the help of two men I have never met—Christopher Tolkien and Humphrey Carpenter. Without their careful and thorough scholarship I could not have begun, much less continued, this book. Deep gratitude goes to Priscilla Tolkien and Owen Barfield, both of whom took time from busy schedules to answer questions, share their insights, and give me valuable criticism. I owe more than thanks to Professor Lewis Lawson, who read the manuscript as it was being written and made me do it over whenever it wasn't right, which was often. Thanks go to Professor Jane Donawerth, who read a book I thought was finished and showed me how it could be improved; to Lisa McCullough, who proofread the book twice, and without whom the index would not have been possible; to Lael Evans Flieger, who also read proof and checked the index one last time. I am grateful to Joe, who pushed, and to Rod, who pulled. And I am enormously grateful for the forbearance of my family, all of whom have lived with this material for the last three years.

Portions of this book were written with the aid of a General Research Board Summer Grant from the University of Maryland.

| PREFACE

In this uneasy century whose people are no more divided from one another than from themselves, when the likelihood of annihilation is the only constant in an age of change, what relevance is to be found in a reactionary English professor's anachronistic flight of fancy about elves and dragons and hobbits and magic jewels? That the books of this "hobbit don," as a skeptical colleague once termed J.R.R. Tolkien, topped the *New York Times* best-seller lists for many weeks only shows the doubters the perennial appeal of escapism and the intellectual sloth of the *hoi polloi*. Tolkien's fiction does not anatomize the empty lives of the middle class nor the squalor and pathos of the poor; it offers no sex (though it has a surprising amount of violence), no social comment, no anger, no alienation. It has, in fact, little or no relationship to (as Oscar Wilde's Gwendolyn puts it) "the actual facts of real life, as we know them."

Gwendolyn is talking about metaphysical speculation, and while Tolkien has a fairly low opinion of real life, and much prefers truth to facts, he would disagree with Gwendolyn that metaphysical speculation is irrelevant to either. The bones of his fiction are exactly such speculation, although they are fleshed with enchantment rather than reality, and clothed in imagination rather than fact.

Why should anyone read Tolkien? For refreshment and entertainment. Why should anyone take his work seriously— as seriously (and that is very serious indeed) as he took it? Because it is tough, uncompromising, honest. Because it confronts directly, albeit imaginatively, those two awkward, embarrassing, even forbidden subjects which our time shrinks from: death, and the relationship between humanity and God. If we do read Tolkien, and if we do take him seriously, we may learn about ourselves—learn much that we did not know and even more than we once knew and have now forgotten.

Tolkien puts us in touch with the supernatural; he opens our eyes to wonder; he gives us, for however brief a period, a universe of beauty and meaning and purpose. Whether there really is such a universe is less important than the undeniable truth that we need one badly, that we are deeply uneasy at the lack of one, and at the prospect that we may have to make, or re-make, one ourselves. Tolkien shows us a way to do that.

Above all, he gives us back words, those tired old counters worn with use, and makes them new again in all their power, variety, and magic. He remembers for us what we have forgotten, that *spell* is both a noun and a verb, that it means incantation as well as the formation of a word by letters, and that to use it in either sense inevitably involves using it in both senses.

If, as Horace maintained, the aim of the poet is to inform and to delight, he will succeed at the former only insofar as he succeeds at the latter. The delight offered by Tolkien—enchantment, poetry (I do not mean verse), vision—engages the imagination while his metaphysical speculation engages the intellect. The questions Tolkien raises are the same ones mankind has always asked: where do we fit in? what do we mean? why are we here? Mythology is as proper a forum for such questions as is philosophy, and while philosophies come and go, mythologies tend to endure as stories long after they have ceased to command belief. Tolkien's mythology enriches, re-evaluates, and melds the great mythologies of Western man. It takes up the established patterns of mythic thought and turns them so that they catch new light. Tolkien's achievement in letters is distinguished, both in fiction and in scholarship. As for the relevance of his work to the twentieth century, he may well turn out to be its greatest mythographer, its greatest exponent of myth, of the songs and stories of the old times, of the tales of how we and the world came to be, and why we need each other. In a world too long deprived of myth, that is no small achievement.

VERLYN FLIEGER
August 1983

| INTRODUCTION

The Silmarillion is without doubt Tolkien's most difficult and perplexing work. As fiction it lacks the hobbit earthiness that grounds *The Lord of the Rings*, as well as that book's moment-to-moment sense of excitement and danger. As fantasy it transcends sword and sorcery to become a vehicle for theological exploration and speculation. Where *The Lord of the Rings* is a tale of adventure with mythic overtones, *The Silmarillion* is myth outright. As part of Tolkien's canon the book is difficult to fit in with Tolkien's other fiction due to the confusing chronology of its composition and publication. Finally, its real significance is the subject of debate, and is far from resolved at this writing. Just how important is *The Silmarillion* in relation to *The Lord of the Rings* and *The Hobbit*? Is it Tolkien's definitive statement, a major contribution to English letters, as its defenders maintain? Or is it inflated, tedious, far inferior to his other work, as its critics suggest? Has the enormous popularity of *The Lord of the Rings* unfairly obscured its real value? Or does it ride on the coattails of its predecessor? Is it the major work or merely background material?

These and other questions have been and will continue to be raised as the debate goes on. Some can be answered now; others must wait for the dust to settle, and for more of Tolkien's myth to emerge. For *The Silmarillion* as we have it is only a part of the mass of material which Tolkien left unpublished at his death and which is being edited and published in segments by his youngest son and literary executor, Christopher Tolkien. To date we have *The Silmarillion* proper—one volume containing a coherent sequence of stories from creation to a brief re-telling of the War of the Ring—and *Unfinished Tales*, a second volume which is exactly what its title implies—uncompleted bits and pieces in which editorial comment sometimes outweighs the text. And there is more to come.* Enough has been published, however, to make critical consideration worthwhile; it seems doubtful that the yet-unpublished material will substantially alter or contradict our perception of what we now have.

The history of the composition of Tolkien's *mythos*, its temporal relationship to his other fiction, and his difficulties in negotiating for its publication are presented with admirable clarity by Humphrey Carpenter in his *Tolkien: A Biography*, and the reader is referred to that book for details.[1] Suffice it to say here that The Silmarillion was written before, during, and after both *The Hobbit* and *The Lord of the Rings*, and that it subsumed *The Hobbit* and engulfed *The Lord of the Rings*, turning the latter from a *Hobbit* sequel into an extension of the larger mythology.

Tolkien's own description of his design is still the best. Writing to Milton Waldman of Collins publishing house, Tolkien explained his vision:

> Do not laugh! But once upon a time (my crest has long since fallen) I had a mind to make a body of more or less connected legend, ranging from the large and cosmogonic, to the level of romantic fairy-story—the larger founded on the lesser in contact with the earth, the lesser drawing splendour from the vast backcloths— which I could dedicate simply to: England; to my country. . . . I would draw some of the great tales in fullness, and leave many only placed in the scheme and sketched. The cycle would be linked to a majestic whole, and yet

---

*Tolkien worked on his mythology for more than fifty years, during which time it acquired unplanned additions, such as ents and hobbits, and the myth had to be adjusted to fit them in. *The Silmarillion, Unfinished Tales, The Hobbit,* and *The Lord of the Rings* are now to be seen as parts of the same body of material that makes up the creation and continuing history of Tolkien's fictive world. To simplify references and to emphasize the wholeness of the concept I will refer to separate volumes by title, but will refer to the whole corpus generically as The Silmarillion.

[1]Humphrey Carpenter, *Tolkien: A Biography* (Boston: Houghton Mifflin, 1977). Hereafter page references will be cited in the text, with this abbreviation: *TAB*.

leave scope for other minds and hands, wielding paint and music and drama. Absurd.[2]

This passage tells as much about the man who wrote it as it does about the work itself. The tone of mixed hope and diffidence, the deprecating "Do not laugh" and "Absurd" reveal a sensibility braced for ridicule. Tolkien was plainly both eager and afraid to expose his dream, fearful that what he once described to his publisher Stanley Unwin as "private and beloved nonsense" (*TLOT*, p. 26) would be misunderstood or made fun of. Yet his words belie his feelings. All that is known about Tolkien—the evidence of his works, his letters, the picture that emerges from Carpenter's biography—makes it clear that he did not think his dream was nonsense or that it was absurd, but that he took it very seriously indeed. That being the case, it would profit scholars and students of Tolkien's work to follow his lead, to take his myth seriously and to enter into it with sympathy and understanding. For it was his lifework, *The Lord of the Rings* notwithstanding. It was the work nearest to his heart, and as Christopher Tolkien points out in the Foreword to *The Silmarillion*, it became over the course of time "the vehicle and depository of his profoundest reflections."[3]

Aside from what is revealed about Tolkien himself, the most striking aspect of his description is the sheer size and reach of the project, the "body of more or less connected legend," the range from the cosmogonic to fairy tale, the "vast backcloths." To be sure, this is a fair description of the makeup of most primary mythologies, those real bodies of connected legend—Hebrew, Norse, Celtic, Finnish—which were Tolkien's models. But the stories of primary myth are retrieved from ancient documents or strung together out of oral material, painstakingly collected and pieced together by

---

[2]J.R.R. Tolkien, *The Letters of J.R.R. Tolkien*, ed. Humphrey Carpenter with Christopher Tolkien (Boston: Houghton Mifflin, 1981), pp. 144-145. Hereafter page references will be cited parenthetically in the text, with this abbreviation: *TLOT*.

[3]Christopher Tolkien in the Foreward to J.R.R. Tolkien's *The Silmarillion*, ed. Christopher Tolkien (Boston: Houghton Mifflin, 1977), p. 7.

scholars. To conceive such a scheme, to construct a secondary mythology out of a single creative imagination, calls for extraordinary ambition and vision. Even Milton, arguably the greatest mythographer in the English language, did no more than re-tell the existing Christian *mythos*. To find anything remotely paralleling Tolkien's achievement we must go to Blake.* And it is well to remember that Blake's mythology was met with incomprehension and a certain critical reserve when it first appeared.

However ambitious the project, Tolkien brought it off. It took him the better part of fifty years, for he began in 1917 with a handwritten notebook titled "The Book of Lost Tales," and was still re-working the stories in 1973, the year he died. The result is very much what he described to Waldman: a body of myth, legend, folktale, and song enriched by the addition of *The Lord of the Rings*, and even (in unintentional imitation of primary mythologies) collated, edited, and published in bits and pieces.

When he wrote to Waldman in 1950, Tolkien was negotiating with Collins publishing house for joint publication of *The Lord of the Rings* and The Silmarillion. Publishers seemed enthusiastic about the one, but cautious or even negative about the other. Tolkien felt strongly that the two works were tied together, and that the history of the Ring rested on the earlier work, indeed, that it was its "continuation and completion, requiring the *Silmarillion* to be fully intelligible" (*TLOT*, pp. 136-137). But beyond that, he was afraid that if The Silmarillion were not published with *The Lord of the Rings*, it would not be published at all.

For a long time it seemed that Tolkien's fears were justified. The projected arrangement with Collins fell through;

---

*The omission of Spenser from these comparisons requires explanation, for *The Lord of the Rings* has been likened to *The Faerie Queene*, and there are striking parallels in aim, in subject matter, and in meaning between Spenser's great work and Tolkien's mythology. However, Spenser's *mythos*, unlike Tolkien's, is consciously and avowedly derived from other authors—from Ariosto, Tasso, Virgil, Ovid, Homer, as well as from Arthurian romance. Furthermore, Spenser's tale is deliberately allegorical, whereas Tolkien's is allusive, suggesting relationships and resonances of meaning without striving for one-to-one correlation.

publishing costs increased; no publisher would undertake so long a work as the joint Silmarillion and *The Lord of the Rings*. Finally, Allen and Unwin, who had published *The Hobbit*, brought out *The Lord of the Rings* separately. For twenty-some years it was read and understood as an independent work. This has caused and still causes critical difficulties, and has contributed in large measure to the confusion over the relative importance of the two works. Critics lauding the richness of Tolkien's world and the detailed texture of its background did not altogether realize that what they had was only one enlarged corner of a vast canvas, a corner meaningful in itself but infinitely more meaningful as part of and contributory to a whole. The book's appendices hinted at early history, and rumors of unpublished mythic material circulated, but scholars and ordinary readers alike had to take *The Lord of the Rings* as it stood. This was not disastrous, but it was certainly unfortunate, for it deprived readers of the heart of the matter. The *ethos* of Tolkien's world was missing. The genesis and history, the religious and philosophical basis, the governing principles of Tolkien's world are explicit in The Silmarillion, implicit in *The Lord of the Rings*. Without the one, the other could not exist.

The importance of this cannot be emphasized too strongly. To read *The Lord of the Rings*, or even better, to re-read it, in the light of *The Silmarillion* is to be newly aware of immensely greater perspective, of a suddenly increased depth of field. Obscure references assume meaning; shadowy figures leap into prominence. *The Lord of the Rings* now clearly has what Tolkien had planned for it, that same illusion of depth which he found and praised in *Beowulf*, the illusion of "surveying a past ... noble and fraught with a deep significance—a past which itself had depth and reached backward into a dark antiquity of sorrow."[4] The tale is now placed in a history, and what had seemed digressions of little

---

[4]J.R.R. Tolkien, "*Beowulf*: The Monsters and the Critics," from *Proceedings of the British Academy*, XXII (London: Oxford University Press, 1937), 245-295. Reprinted in *An Anthology of Beowulf Criticism*, ed. Lewis E. Nicholson (South Bend, Ind.: University of Notre Dame Press, 1963), p. 80.

relevance are now seen to be essential elements of plot and theme.

The irony in all this is that without the separate and prior publication of *The Lord of the Rings*, there would have been no audience for *The Silmarillion*. Without familiarity with Middle-earth and hobbits, without the drama of the Ring, readers would not have been prepared for the more complex and rarefied *Silmarillion*. Enthusiasm and interest, appetites whetted by over two decades of waiting for more, created a ready-made readership for *The Silmarillion* when it appeared in 1977.

Even so, the initial reception for Tolkien's mythology was mixed, and, in a furtherance of the irony, mixed precisely because *The Lord of the Rings* had set up expectations which it was never the intent of *The Silmarillion* to fulfill. Readers eager to re-inhabit the world of the Shire and Fangorn Forest were instead given an abstruse creation myth, lists of gods and goddesses with explanations of their various functions, and a confusing proliferation of names and genealogies with no readily apparent import. Many lovers of Tolkien were put off; many were downright bored. Hopes for romance and high adventure, for Tolkien's signature combination of epic and earthiness were damped by biblical language and a narrative constructed along the lines of the Old Testament.

Reviewers and critics seemed not quite to know what to make of what they had. *Time* magazine, while conceding that some of *The Silmarillion* was "majestic," called the rest "at least half fustian and more than a yard long," and decided that Tolkien's prose sounded like "a parody of Edgar Rice Burroughs in the style of the *Book of Revelation*."[5] The *New York Review of Books* predicted that there would be "far more purchasers of the new volume than ever read it through," and suggested that had it been published first, "it might well have laid a blight on the entire series."[6]

---

[5]Timothy Foote, "Middle-earth *Genesis*," *Time*, Oct. 24, 1977, p. 120.

[6]Robert M. Adams, "The Hobbit Habit," *New York Review of Books*, Nov. 24, 1977, p. 22.

Not all comment was negative. There were those who understood what Tolkien was attempting, and had sympathy for his aim and admired his achievement. The *Washington Post Book World* carried Joseph McLellan's review on its front page under the perceptive title "Frodo and the Cosmos." McLellan correctly saw the relationship between *The Lord of the Rings* and *The Silmarillion,* and saw also how completely the former work had overshadowed the latter:

> . . . Tolkien found an enthusiastic audience for one small corner of his massive vision and no market at all for the greater part of his imaginings. And like a true professional . . . he adapted—shrank—his vision to suit the available market. One is reminded of Shakespeare, whose magnificent series of historical plays produced, offhand and almost by accident, a minor character named Falstaff. . . .[7]

Another who understood Tolkien's vision (though he could not praise it without qualification) was John Gardner, whose lengthy comments in the *New York Times Book Review* explored fully what he called "the eccentric heroism of Tolkien's attempt."[8] As a medievalist, Gardner was well-equipped to understand the central concepts of Tolkien's myth and the forces which shape his cosmos. He came very near the mark when he asserted, "Music is the central symbol and the total myth of 'The Silmarillion,' a symbol that becomes interchangeable with light (music's projection)" (WT, p. 39). These are indeed the central ideas; Gardner is mistaken only in calling them symbols. It is the essence of Tolkien's world that they are neither symbols nor metaphors, but actualities to be taken literally. But Gardner knew the medieval background and the medieval world-view, and he reached the heart of Tolkien's myth when he said:

---

[7]Joseph McLellan, "Frodo and the Cosmos," *Washington Post Book World,* Sept. 4, 1977, Sec. E, p. 3.

[8]John Gardner, "The World of Tolkien," *New York Times Book Review,* Oct. 23, 1977, p. 40. Hereafter page references will be cited parenthetically in the text, with this abbreviation: WT.

What is medieval in Tolkien's vision is his set of organizing principles, his symbolism and his pattern of legends and events. In the work of Boëthius and the
scholastic philosophers, as in Dante and Chaucer, musical harmony is the first principle of cosmic balance,
and the melody of individuals—the expression of individual free will—is the standard figure for the play
of free will within the overall design of Providence.
This concord of will and overall design was simultaneously expressed, in medieval thought, in terms of
light: the foundation of music was the orderly tuning
of the spheres. Other lights—lights borrowed from the
cosmic originals—came to be important in exegetical
writings and of course in medieval poetry: famous jewels or works in gold and silver were regularly symbolic
of the order that tests individual will. . . . (WT, p. 40)

Nonetheless, Gardner had reservations about *The Silmarillion*, and as reader rather than scholar he clearly pre-
ferred *The Lord of the Rings*, saying that it "looms already
as one of the truly great works of the human spirit, giving
luster to its less awesome but still miraculous satellites, 'The
Hobbit' and now 'The Silmarillion' " (WT, p. 1). Gardner seems
to speak for the general reader. And while there is beginning
to be a modest body of scholarship devoted to *The Silmarillion*, critical opinion seems still to be weighted in favor of
The Lord of the Rings.

Of the work that has been done, Randel Helms's *Tolkien
and the Silmarils* gives a useful general overview of *The Silmarillion.*[9] Jane Chance Nitzsche devotes a brief final chapter
to it in *Tolkien's Art: A "Mythology for England."* Her focus,
however, is on Tolkien's other fiction, including the minor
works, and she frankly admits that she finds *The Silmarillion*
"difficult to read and even more difficult to enjoy." She suggests that it might be viewed as "an early and even minor
work," perhaps best understood as a source for and influence

---

[9]Randel Helms, *Tolkien and the Silmarils* (n.p.: Houghton Mifflin,
1981).

on Tolkien's later fiction.[10] This cannot be the case. Certainly it is the major influence (within the fictive world) on *The Lord of the Rings*, and it is undeniably the source of all its history. But it is hardly a minor work, unless the Old Testament, source for and influence on the New Testament, can be called a minor work. *The Silmarillion* precedes and prepares for *The Lord of the Rings*, but both are parts of a continuous story, pieces of that "body of more or less connected legend" of which *The Silmarillion* is unmistakably the "cosmogonic," while *The Lord of the Rings* is in relation to it "the lesser in contact with the earth," drawing its splendor from *The Silmarillion*'s "vast backcloths."

One important benefit that knowledge of *The Silmarillion* will confer on Tolkien scholarship is the advantage of a better perspective on the relationship of his work to those others with which it is so often compared: the Christian fantasies of C.S. Lewis and Charles Williams.* Much of the early criticism of *The Lord of the Rings* was marked by a tendency to link Tolkien with these two—his fellow Inklings and Oxford companions. The basis of this seems to have been their known friendship with one another, their shared Christian-

---

[10]Jane Chance Nitzsche, *Tolkien's Art* (London: MacMillan Press, 1979), p. 3.

*See, for example, William Irwin's "There and Back Again: The Romances of Williams, Lewis, and Tolkien," in *Sewanee Review*, LXIX (Fall 1961), 566-578; Charles Moorman's *The Precincts of Felicity: The Augustinian City of the Oxford Christians* (Gainesville: University of Florida Press, 1966); R. J. Reilly's *Romantic Religion: A Study of Barfield, Lewis, Williams, and Tolkien* (Athens: University of Georgia Press, 1971); Roger Sale's "England's Parnassus: C.S. Lewis, Charles Williams, and J. R. R. Tolkien," in *Hudson Review*, XVII (Summer 1964), 203-225; Gunnar Urang's *Shadows of Heaven: Religion and Fantasy in the Writing of Clive Staples Lewis, Charles Williams and John Ronald Reuel Tolkien* (London: S.C.M. Press, 1971); Marjorie Wright's "The Cosmic Kingdom of Myth: A Study in the Myth-philosophy of Charles Williams, C. S. Lewis and J. R. R. Tolkien," unpublished doctoral dissertation, University of Illinois, 1960, from which comes her article "The Vision of Cosmic Order in the Oxford Mythmakers," in *Imagination and the Spirit: Essays in Literature and the Christian Faith Presented to Clyde S. Kilby*, ed. Charles A. Huttar (Grand Rapids, Mich.: Eerdmans, 1971), pp. 259-276.

ity, and superficial similarities in their use of fantasy as a fictional mode. The critical impulse was to link all three as religious fantasy writers with a common goal, a kind of unofficial Christian brotherhood of craftsmen. That this was never the case is made plain by Humphrey Carpenter, who devotes a chapter of his book on the Inklings to investigating, carefully considering, and finally dismissing the idea.[11] Carpenter's conclusion is that the Inklings were a highly informal group with a somewhat shifting population who shared interests and ideas, but had no sense of mission nor any common goal. Nevertheless, the notion of similarity dies hard, and Middle-earth is still compared with Narnia and Logres. *The Silmarillion* provides needed evidence that as a Christian writer Tolkien is distinct from Lewis and Williams, far more unlike them than he is like.

As developed in *The Silmarillion*, Tolkien's Christianity is manifestly tougher and darker than Lewis's, less mystical and occult than Williams's, and far less hopeful than either man's faith. Tolkien's Christian belief is precarious, constantly renewed yet always in jeopardy, and it is this precariousness which gives his work its knife-edge excitement. The issue is always in doubt. Where Lewis's Christianity is firmly based in logic, and Williams's in a sense of mystical practice, Tolkien's Christianity is measured against experience and constantly put to the test.

Moreover, *The Silmarillion* can be described as Christian only in the broadest, most general sense, and in no sense can *The Lord of the Rings* be given so specific a label. That both works are informed with the spirit of Christianity is clear. But the seeker after Christian reference (as distinct from Christian meaning) will find little or nothing—especially in *The Lord of the Rings*—to get a grip on. This is no accident; it is Tolkien's stated intent. "I have not put in," he said, "or have cut out, practically all references to anything like 'religion', to cults or practices, in the imaginary world. For the

---

[11]Humphrey Carpenter, *The Inklings* (Boston: Houghton Mifflin, 1979). Chapter Four of Part Three, "A Fox That Isn't There," examines the fellowship.

religious element is absorbed into the story and the symbolism" (*TLOT*, p. 172). Other statements Tolkien made clarify his reasons for this, and do much to elucidate the essential difference between his use of myth and that of Lewis and Williams. The same letter to Milton Waldman which describes his mythology for England states his position on religion in myth: "Myth and fairy-story must, as all art, reflect and contain in solution elements of moral and religious truth (or error), but not explicit, not in the known form of the primary 'real' world" (*TLOT*, p. 144).

So, for example, there is in what we have of Tolkien's mythology no explicit Christ-episode such as the sacrificial death and resurrection of Aslan in Lewis's *The Lion, the Witch, and the Wardrobe.* There is no Graal, as in Williams's *War in Heaven,* and no overt Christianity, as in his Arthurian poems. *The Silmarillion* is Tolkien's gloss on Christianity, illustrating its universals, not its specifics. It is concerned, he says, "with Fall, Mortality, and the Machine" (*TLOT*, p. 145), subjects which, in the broadest sense, are the concern of all myths in all ages.

Independent though he is of Lewis and Williams, Tolkien manifests a surprising similarity of thought with the "other Inkling," the less known, less popular, but perhaps most influential of all—Owen Barfield, the unobtrusive fourth of the big three. Barfield is not a fantasist; he is a speculative Christian thinker and philosopher whose interest lies chiefly in the relationship between myth and language. Barfield's theory of the interdependence of myth and language was perhaps the most direct influence (saving the *Beowulf* poet) on Tolkien's myth.* Certainly it is very much present in Tolkien's

---

*The relationship between Barfield's work and Tolkien's is explored in Chapter III of the present book. Evidence that Tolkien was aware of it can be found in his reference to Barfield in a letter, dated 31 August, 1937, written to C. A. Furth of Allen and Unwin, publishers of *The Hobbit.* "The only philological remark (I think) in *The Hobbit* is on p. 221 (lines 6-7 from end): an odd mythological way of referring to linguistic philosophy, and a point that will (happily) be missed by any who have not read Barfield (few have), and probably by those who have" (*TLOT*, p. 22).

fictive assumption that myth and language create one another. And Barfield's theory is central to the thesis of this book: that the polarities of light and dark, perceived through and expressed in language, define one another and develop Tolkien's world.

The Silmarillion and *The Lord of the Rings* are parts of a whole, made separate by publication's exigencies and delays. But separated though they have been, they derive from and express the same stupendous vision—Tolkien's strangely orthodox, highly unorthodox, ultra-Christian, extra-Christian exercise in imaginative creation. *The Silmarillion* can be fully understood without reference to *The Lord of the Rings*, but the reverse is not true. Any attempt to read, to understand, to evaluate Tolkien's fiction and his contribution to twentieth-century fantasy and theological speculation should begin where he began—at the beginning. Only then can there be an understanding of where he is going, and, even more important, why he is going there.

Splintered Light

I
A MAN OF ANTITHESES

I perceived or thought of the Light of God and in it suspended one small mote (or millions of motes to only one of which was my small mind directed), glittering white because of the individual ray from the Light which both held and lit it. (Not that there were individual rays issuing from the Light, but the mere existence of the mote and its position in relation to the Light was in itself a line, and the line was Light). And the ray was the Guardian Angel of the mote, not a thing interposed between God and the creature, but God's very attention itself, personalized.

TOLKIEN IN A LETTER TO HIS SON CHRISTOPHER

. . . if there is a God. . . .

TOLKIEN IN A LETTER TO HIS SON MICHAEL

Both these statements, antithetical though they may seem, are typical of Tolkien. They were written at different times, in letters to different sons, and obviously motivated by different circumstances and different thoughts. What is typical is not just the different message of each, but the distance between them as well, the enormous shift of mood that led Humphrey Carpenter to describe Tolkien as "a man of antitheses" (*TAB*, p. 95). The illuminating, otherworldly beauty of the first and the bleak doubt of the second are evidence of extreme shifts in outlook, oscillation between hope and despair. The man who wrote them knew the heights and the depths. This is not to say that such shifts of mood are unique to Tolkien; the road between belief and doubt is one traveled in both directions at one time or another by many thinking

Christians. But Tolkien's statements betoken something more than brief moments of belief and doubt: they are emblematic of the poles of his emotional life. Even more, they are the boundary markers of his worlds—both the world he perceived around him and the world he created in his fiction.

No careful reader of Tolkien's work can fail to be aware of the polarities of light and dark which give it form and tension. His work is built on contrast—between hope and despair, good and evil, enlightenment and ignorance—and these contrasts are embodied in the polarity of light and dark which is the creative outgrowth of his contrary moods, the "antitheses" of his nature. Carpenter called him a man of extreme contrasts who was "never moderate; love, intellectual enthusiasm, distaste, anger, self-doubt, guilt, laughter, each was in his mind exclusively and in full force when he experienced it . . ." (*TAB,* p. 129).

Carpenter's biography suggests that these contrasts are traceable to certain formative events in Tolkien's early years: specifically to the death of his father when he was four—which led to an unusually close relationship with his mother—and to her unexpected, sudden death when he was twelve. These events seem to have laid the foundation for Tolkien's mercurial shifts of feeling. Most important, his feeling for his mother was deeply connected to his lifelong devotion to his religion.

Mabel Tolkien's conversion to Catholicism when Tolkien was eight years old permanently estranged her from her relatives. Her determination to bring up her children—Tolkien and his younger brother Hilary—in the Catholic faith cut her off from the emotional and financial support of her family. Tolkien came to feel that his mother's heroic efforts to raise and educate her sons alone had drained her strength, and were the direct cause of her death. When she died he was bereft. "The loss of his mother," says Carpenter, "had a profound effect on his personality. It made him into a pessimist. Or rather, it made him into two people." Carpenter goes on to characterize Tolkien's two sides:

> He was by nature a cheerful almost irrepressible person
> with a great zest for life. . . . But from now onwards
> there was to be a second side, more private but pre-
> dominant in his diaries and letters. This side of him
> was capable of bouts of profound despair. More pre-
> cisely, and more closely related to his mother's death,
> when he was in this mood he had a deep sense of im-
> pending loss. Nothing was safe. Nothing would last.
> No battle would be won forever. (*TAB*, p. 31)

His solace was his religion. But these feelings colored his
religious outlook and gave it the same mixture of light and
dark. "My own dear mother was a martyr indeed," he wrote,
"and it is not to everyone that God grants so easy a way to
his great gifts as he did to Hilary and myself, giving us a
mother who killed herself with labour and trouble to ensure
us keeping the faith" (*TAB*, p. 31). Tolkien's description of
his mother's sacrifice as an "easy" way to God is hard to
fathom, for it is clear that the shock of his mother's death
affected him deeply. And yet the statement is evidence of the
close, emotional association which he always made between
his mother and his faith. This is more than polarity; it is
paradox. His Catholicism was inextricably linked with his
mother, but her adherence to that religion had, in his view,
led to her death and thus to his bereavement. The very thing
which gave him his faith robbed him of his mother, and thus
mixed with that faith a sense of irretrievable loss.

The same contrast is apparent here which marks the two
quotations heading this chapter, that contrast which led to
Carpenter's description of Tolkien as two people—one a naturally cheerful man, the other pessimistic and despairing. But
this may be too simple a description of the complexity of
feeling which Tolkien experienced and which his work reflects. For these feelings found a Christian context in Tolkien's Catholic view of the world as fallen and of man as
imperfect. Pessimism is simply disappointed optimism, but
a Christian acceptance of the Fall of Man leads inevitably to
the idea that imperfection is the state of things in this world,
and that human actions—however hopeful—cannot rise above

imperfection. "Actually I am a Christian," Tolkien wrote of himself, "and indeed a Roman Catholic, so that I do not expect 'history' to be anything but a 'long defeat'—though it contains (and in a legend may contain more clearly and movingly) some samples or glimpses of final victory" (*TLOT*, p. 255). The world, then, must be seen as a place of defeat and disappointment, and man must be seen as born to trouble as the sparks fly upward. Tolkien's enclosure of the word "history" in quotation marks suggests that he means history to contrast with eternity, and that the "long defeat" has to do with humanity's work in this world, not its expectations of the next.

All this adds up to an outlook both psychological and religious in which the one can hardly be separated from the other, an outlook based on the sense of expulsion from both a private and a communal Eden. Tolkien's pull toward the dark springs from his personal sense of loss, but is coupled with his acceptance of mankind's exile from the Garden. His world is shadowed by its past as well as his past, lighted only by the vision of the white Light which holds the mote. That vision of the Light remains a vision—a Grail to be sought but never grasped by fallen man in a fallen world.

This alternation between the vision of hope and the knowledge of despair—between light and dark—is both the essence of Tolkien and the clearest characteristic of his work. The contrast and interplay of light and dark are essential elements of his fiction. The light/dark polarity operates on all levels—literal, metaphoric, symbolic. It engenders Creation and Fall; it becomes language; and its interplay becomes the interplay of good and evil, belief and doubt, free will and fate. But while light and dark are both present in Tolkien's fiction, the emotional weight is on the dark side. The presence and power of the dark are among the most effective elements in his mythology. For his vision of the light rides on his knowledge of the dark as sound rides on silence, as the spoken word rides on pause and hesitation—each needs the other. The shadow defines and thereby reveals the light as the brightness of the light sharpens the shadow. Opposite points on the circle, they are held in tension by

simultaneous attraction and repulsion. Their mutual interdependence embodies all of the polarities in Tolkien's theme,
for as light cannot be known without darkness, so hope needs
the contrast of despair to give it meaning, and free will op-
poses the concept of fate.

Tolkien's medium for all of this is words, a point so obvious that it may seem absurd to make a note of it. But it is
important to remember that all of Tolkien's studies, the focus
of his profession, was a concentration on the importance of
the word. His profession as philologist and his vocation as
writer of fantasy/theology overlapped and mutually sup-
ported one another. For Tolkien, appreciation and understanding of any text depended on properly understanding the words,
their literal meaning and their historical development. They
are important as the expression of an author, but just as important as manifestations of the outlook of a culture and an
age. We truly know a text only when we understand the
words as they were used in the time the text was composed.
Only then is it possible to touch the minds of the author and
of his audience, to bridge the temporal distance between that
time and our own.

Tolkien's scholarship is founded on this principle. His
professional work is in the service of the word, and we may
expect his creative work to be likewise. His scholarship gives
a clearer view of this, and any sampling of his scholarly articles will make the point. As often as not, his work served
to reveal a hitherto unnoticed or unappreciated aspect of a
text. A good example is his essay "Chaucer as a Philologist:
The Reeve's Tale," a seventy-page investigation (he apolo-
gizes for its skimpiness!) of Chaucer's use of northern dialect
to characterize the two clerks in *The Reeve's Tale*. This use
of dialect, heretofore unnoticed and remarked only as incon-
sistency in spelling, was explained by Tolkien as a deliberate
departure from a norm of speech. Chaucer, he suggested, was
consciously putting regional dialect into the mouths of two
characters for comic and satiric effect. When the clerks, who
have been stereotyped as country bumpkins, turn the tables
on the Miller—seducing his wife and daughter in retaliation
for his theft of their grain—the story is more than simply a

case of the biter bit. With the addition of dialect, it becomes a case of country mice getting back at the town mouse and upholding the shrewdness of the provinces against the pseudo-sophistication of city slickers.

The value of this to illuminate the humor of the tale and Chaucer's skill at his craft is obvious. Beyond this, Tolkien's essay makes the point that Chaucer's London audience was familiar enough with northern dialect to recognize it and appreciate the joke. Awareness of this gives the modern reader of Chaucer an idea of regional differences of speech in four-teenth-century England, as well as a glimpse of how those regions perceived one another—much as a modern dialect joke will reveal not only the character of its actors but the attitudes and perceptions of the teller and his audience.

Such conscious use of regional speech, said Tolkien, could have been made only by "a man interested in language and consciously observant of it."[1] The description could serve as well for Tolkien as for Chaucer. Indeed, the title of the essay makes it clear that one philologist is studying and learning from another. It takes one to know one. Not just Chaucer's practice of the craft but Tolkien's own use of it to reveal additional meaning underscore the importance of studying, understanding, and appreciating the word. Tolkien's goal, as he explained it in his essay, was to "recover the detail" of what Chaucer wrote, even "down to forms and spellings, to recapture an idea of what it sounded like, to make certain what it meant."[2] The key words here are "recover" and "re-capture," with their treasure-hunter's sense of discovering lost riches. In getting back Chaucer's original intent we ex-perience as fully as possible Chaucer's meaning as understood by his audience in his time.

Tolkien did not keep his knowledge in compartments; his scholarly expertise informs his creative work. He uses re-gional, cultural, and psychological variations in language with telling effect in his fiction. One can imagine a seventy-page

---

[1] J.R.R. Tolkien, "Chaucer as a Philologist: *The Reeve's Tale*," *Trans-actions of the Philological Society* (London: David Nutt, 1934), p. 3.

[2] Tolkien, "Chaucer," p. 1.

essay centuries hence on "Tolkien as a Philologist: *The Lord of the Rings.*" In that work Tolkien carefully differentiates between the more urbane speech of the Took, Baggins, and Brandybuck hobbits and the rural dialect of the Gamgees and the Cottons. Elven speech is liquid, musical; elven diction is formal and archaic. Orc speech is harsh and gutteral; orc diction is street slang. Strider's language is plainer and more direct than the epic diction and syntax of Aragorn—a nice touch, since both are the same man, and the change in language signals the transition from Ranger to King. Gollum's childish (occasionally child-*like*), schizophrenic whinings and mutterings mark him as infantile and regressive, almost divorced from the human community. Even Tolkien's love relationships are conveyed through nuances of speech rather than by narrative description. The infatuated Eowyn addresses Aragorn with the intimate "thou," while he is careful to keep her at a distance with the formal "you."

Tolkien's fascination with language goes beyond dialect to focus on the meanings and resonances of specific words as they illuminate a culture and that culture's perception. His essay *"Sigelwara Land"* is an extended gloss on the use of the Old English word *Sigelwaran* or *Sigelhearwan* for Æthiops in Old English glosses of Latin texts and in other Old English writings. Here he combines philological skill with his own special imaginative sympathy for words to come up with an educated guess about Old English mythic perception.[3]

He establishes that the word in question, *Sigelhearwa,* must have existed as an independent term before the appearance of the Greek Æthiops in language and literature both as word and as concept. On the basis of this he suggests that *Sigelhearwa* is the preservation of "at least a name, if no more, from the vanished native mythology or its borderland of half-mythical geography" (SL, p. 192). He goes on to say

---

[3]J.R.R. Tolkien, *"Sigelwara Land,"* Part I, *Medium Aevum,* 1 (Dec. 1932), pp. 183-196. *"Sigelwara Land,"* Part II, *Medium Aevum,* 3 (June 1934), pp. 95-111. Both parts published by Basil Blackwell in Oxford. Hereafter page references will be cited parenthetically in the text, with this abbreviation: SL.

that the word must, *"as a whole,* have meant . . . something like 'black people living in a hot region'—whether as a rumour of the actual races of Africa, or as a memory of some mythical *Muspells megir* [in Norse myth the region of fiery sparks] of realms of fire, or both . . ." (SL, p. 193).

Tolkien's analysis of the separate meaning of the word's two elements finds *sigel,* "sun," blended with the homonym *sigel/sigle,* "jewel," to convey a possible perception of the sun as a jewel and jewels as sun-like. The one word might easily carry both meanings without necessarily being specific about either. *Hearwa* is connected to Gothic *haúri,* "coal," Old Norse *hyr-r,* "fire," and related to Old English *heorþ* and *hier-stan,* "roast." This evidence suggests that the two elements combined would convey a concept something like "sunjewel-burned" or "jewelsun-roasted" people. Tolkien suggests an Old English perception of black Africans as conflated with figures or concepts from Norse mythology, and thus seen as "rather the sons of Muspell than of Ham, the ancestors of the *Silhearwan* with red-hot eyes that emitted sparks, with faces black as soot" (SL, p. 110).

Since the essay combines philology with a leap of imagination, Tolkien is honest enough to call his conclusions "guesswork" seeking to "probe a past probably faded even before the earliest documents . . . which now preserve mention of the *Sigelhearwan* were written." Yet, he goes on to say in defense of his guesswork, "it may not be pointless to have probed. Glimpses are caught, if dim and confused, of the background of English and northern tradition and imagination . . ." (SL, p. 111). Where "recover" and "recapture" characterized the Chaucer essay, the key word here is "imagination," which shows plainly that the reward for Tolkien in such a painstaking and (it must be admitted) obscure piece of research is the penetration into a lost attitude of mind, the participation of the imaginative faculty of a people long gone.

In both essays Tolkien follows the word as far back as he can take it, back to an early use by an author or the early appearance in a text. It is a voyage to recover meaning and from that meaning to recapture the imagination and perception of those for whom the word was current. This careful precision joined with imaginative sympathy is typical of his scholarship and is also an important element in his creative work. In his own use of words he strives always for the same exactitude and richness of meaning which he seeks to recapture for earlier authors. For his scholarship, combined with imagination, is the matrix of his fiction. Research into early forms and uses of words, the search after lost meanings and nuances—a scientific study in the truest sense of the word—led him through science into art, and through art into an almost spiritual realm wherein the word was the conveyer of primal truth, the magic vehicle not just of communication but of genuine communion. As such, words were for Tolkien not just a window onto the past but the key to that lost relationship between man and God of which our sense of the Fall is our only memory. Words are the clearest record of the "long defeat" of which he wrote, and we can imagine that he saw them also as the vehicle for the "glimpses of final victory" for which he hoped. C.S. Lewis's comment that Tolkien "had been inside language" (*TAB*, p. 134) was thus no figure of speech, but the literal truth. He had been inside the word, had experienced its power and seen with its perception.

Others who knew Tolkien came to much the same conclusion. Simonne d'Ardenne, one of Tolkien's Oxford students and herself a philologist, found another way to put it. In an essay called "The Man and the Scholar," her contribution to the memorial volume *J.R.R. Tolkien: Scholar and Storyteller*, Mlle. d'Ardenne recalled saying to him once, apropos his work: "You broke the veil, didn't you, and passed through?" and she adds that he "readily admitted" having done so.[4] Her question is not in the usual mode of philological inquiry, nor is his reply. Both question and answer betoken an awareness and acceptance of the word as one avenue into the perception of the super-natural, the super-real. To break the veil and pass through would be to penetrate beyond

---

[4]S.T.R.O. d'Ardenne, "The Man and the Scholar," in *J.R.R. Tolkien: Scholar and Storyteller—Essays in Memoriam*, ed. Mary Salu and Robert T. Farrell (Ithaca: Cornell University Press, 1979), p. 34.

normal human perception into another, perhaps higher reality, one always present but not readily accessible.

For Tolkien to admit to such an experience implies that he felt that his use of the word as well as his study of it had carried him beyond invention into a real vision of that which he wrote, that the word itself was the light by which he saw. This implicit correlation of word and light became explicit in his critical writing, most notably in the theory of sub-creation that he introduced in his essay "On Fairy-stories."* Other statements Tolkien made carry the same message. He writes of "reporting" and "recording" the events of *The Lord of the Rings*, and refers to the time when he was writing it as a period when the story "was beginning to unroll itself and to unfold prospects of labour and exploration in yet unknown country. . . ."[5] Of the tales in his mythology he said: "They arose in my mind as 'given' things, and as they came, separately, so too the links grew" (*TAB*, p. 92). In a letter to a reader he explained: "I have long ceased to *invent*. . . . I wait till I seem to know what really happened" (*TLOT*, p. 231).

All of these statements are indicative of one of the most important facets of Tolkien's concept of story in general, and of myth, legend, and fairy tale in particular—that they convey truth rather than fact, and, even more important, that they are the best vehicles for certain kinds of truth. Of myths and legends he wrote, "They must inevitably contain a large measure of ancient wide-spread motives or elements. After all, I believe that legends and myths are largely made of 'truth', and indeed present aspects of it that can only be received in this mode; and long ago certain truths and modes of this kind were discovered and must always reappear" (*TLOT*, p. 147). Certainly he felt that his own tales were true in this sense, and were as much a reappearance of long-ago truths as were myth and legend. It seems clear that for Tolkien the fictive

---

*Mentioned here for clarification, this point warrants further exploration, and will be discussed at length in the following chapter.

[5]J.R.R. Tolkien, *The Tolkien Reader* (New York: Ballantine Books, 1966; rpt. 1979), p. 31.

mode best conveys this kind of truth, bypassing as it does the dissecting intellect to directly touch the imagination and the intuition.

For Tolkien, story is the most effective carrier of truth because it works with images rather than concepts, with forms rather than abstract ideas, and with action rather than argument. It is more effective to show light than to explain it, easier to imagine darkness than to analyze it, simpler and more direct to illustrate through character and event than to expound the relative qualities of hope and despair, belief and doubt, good and evil. And certainly it was easiest of all for one who loved and lived in words to picture light and dark as actualities and allow them to convey their own values. The polarity of light and dark which generates the elements of Tolkien's fictive world and which motivates its action is created, reflected, and conveyed through the power of the word.

That power is, by its nature, the power to change as well as to express. Behind the word is always that which it represents, but above it flickers an evanescent, changing meaning which carries in it the ability to heighten and ultimately to transcend a given definition. There is thus inherent in words the vitality which makes them an effective medium for the transmutation of life into art. What in Tolkien's life was an imbalance in temperament, a contradiction of moods, becomes in his art a supremely controlled balance of forces. The antitheses so clearly manifest in the man become in his myth the paradox which is at once its governing principle and its central mystery. Light and dark are translated from extremes of outlook into equal forces held in tension by their opposition to and dependence upon one another. Major, seemingly unassociated aspects of Tolkien's life—his oscillation between hope and despair, his scholarly absorption in the word, his imaginative capacity—come together in his fiction to show us light and dark at once literal, metaphoric, and symbolic.

II
CATASTROPHE AND EUCATASTROPHE

He is a man, and that for him and for many is sufficient tragedy.

TOLKIEN, ESSAY ON
BEOWULF

. . . and they lived happily ever after.

ANONYMOUS

Tolkien's use of dark and light as emblems of despair and hope is manifest in his criticism as well as in his fiction, but in a somewhat different mode: his criticism uses the words to mediate and explain, where his fiction embodies them and makes them real. Two of Tolkien's major essays, written around the time when the world of hobbits was beginning to weave itself into The Silmarillion, are devoted to exploration of dark and light, and to affirmation of both. Analysis of these essays will lay the groundwork for understanding Tolkien's correlation of light and dark with the language base of his mythology.

"*Beowulf*: The Monsters and the Critics" and "On Fairy-stories"* are different enough in subject matter and treatment

---

*These two articles are fast becoming (as they should be) touchstones in Tolkien criticism, and it is a rare Tolkien scholar who does not refer to one or the other and often both for illumination of the fiction. Among those who use the essays in support of critical points are R.J. Reilly and Jane Chance Nitzsche in the works by those authors already referred to, and Randel Helms, whose Tolkien's World (Boston: Houghton Mifflin, 1974) discusses both essays at some length, as does his book on The Silmarillion.

that they could with some truth be labeled "dark" and "light" respectively. The titles themselves hint that the antitheses so much a part of Tolkien's nature are separated in the essays into discrete components, as the following passages (one from each essay) clearly show:

> When we have read his [the poet's] poem as a poem rather than as a collection of episodes, we perceive that he who wrote *hæ leð under heofenum* may have meant in dictionary terms 'heroes under heaven', or 'mighty men upon earth', but he and his hearers were thinking of the *eormengrund,* the great earth, ringed with *garsecg,* the shoreless sea, beneath the sky's inaccessible roof; whereon, as in a little circle of light about their halls, men with courage as their stay went forward to that battle with the hostile world and the offspring of the dark which ends for all, even the kings and champions, in defeat.[1]

The contrast between this and the next passage, from the fairy-story essay, even though this latter does not specifically name light, could not be more marked:

> The consolation of fairy-stories, the joy of the happy ending: or more correctly of the good catastrophe, the sudden joyous "turn" . . . does not deny the existence of *dyscatastrophe,* of sorrow and failure: the possibility of these is necessary to the joy of deliverance; it denies (in the face of much evidence, if you will) universal final defeat and in so far is *evangelium,* giving a fleeting glimpse of Joy, Joy beyond the walls of the world, poignant as grief.[2]

---

[1] J.R.R. Tolkien, "*Beowulf*: The Monsters and the Critics," in *An Anthology of Beowulf Criticism,* ed. Lewis E. Nicholson (South Bend, Ind.: University of Notre Dame Press, 1963), p. 67. Hereafter page references will be cited parenthetically in the text, with this abbreviation: BMC.

[2] J.R.R. Tolkien, "On Fairy-stories," in *Essays Presented to Charles Williams,* ed. C.S. Lewis (London: Oxford University Press, 1947), pp. 38-39. Reprinted in *Tree and Leaf* (Boston: Houghton Mifflin, 1965). Reprinted in the "Tree and Leaf" section of *The Tolkien Reader* (New York: Ballantine Books, 1966; rpt. 1979), pp. 85-86. Hereafter page references will be cited parenthetically in the text, with this abbreviation: OFS.

Though the contrast is obvious, it would be oversimplification to see these passages, or the essays from which they come, as polar opposites only, without acknowledging that within each is the same opposition of light and dark. Although one speaks movingly about man's defeat by the offspring of the dark, and the other celebrates the joy of the happy ending, each essay contains elements of dark and light held in interdependent tension. The darkness of the first passage needs the little circle of light to give it meaning; the joy of the second passage is consoling only in light of the possibility of sorrow. And the last phrase which calls joy as "poignant as grief" conveys an idea of joy and grief (and thus light and dark) as two halves of the circle, reversed images of one another. What changes from one essay to the other is the emphasis; the balance shifts. In the *Beowulf* essay, dark heavily outweighs light; the heroes go from light into dark and down to defeat. In the fairy-story essay, light is victorious; joy triumphs over sorrow.

The essays are important in two respects. Each is a landmark in its particular field; and each reveals a different aspect of the author and of his fiction. They were composed (within three years of one another) at a time when Tolkien was deeply involved in his mythology. Independent as works of criticism, in the context of one another and of Tolkien's fiction they can be read as informing and informed by his creative work.

Through the *Beowulf* essay Tolkien almost single-handedly reversed the accepted scholarly view of the poem current at the time, a view which held that it was an important but puzzling and seriously flawed piece of work which inexplicably focused on such flights of fancy as monsters; that it was valuable chiefly as a philological and historical artifact. Tolkien defended *Beowulf* as a work of art valuable in its own right. His essay argues that the poem's "flaws" are in reality its glories, that its hero's battles against monsters and his final defeat by a dragon—the hostile offspring of the outer darkness—are in fact the embodiment of the poet's theme.

The fairy-story essay did not reverse a critical trend, but it did begin one. Tolkien was the first reputable scholar since

Aristotle to bend his attention to the development of a critical theory for the evaluation of fantasy. He was certainly the first reputable scholar since the Grimms* to suggest—in public, at any rate—that fairy tales and fantasy were valid literary modes worthy of serious attention. His essay on the nature and function of fairy-stories explores the value and special appeal of this kind of fiction, and sets up solid critical standards for judging it. Like the *Beowulf* essay, the fairy-story essay has become a standard critical text in its field. It is worth noting that each essay made a point of taking seriously a subject which until then had been dismissed as unworthy of scholarship.

The *Beowulf* essay came first. Originally composed as the Sir Israel Gollancz Memorial Lecture, Tolkien delivered it before the British Academy on November 25, 1936. The opening section, a refutation of the current state of criticism, is essentially a defense of monsters—and particularly dragons—as serious subject matter. For Tolkien, battle with monsters and eventual defeat by them is what gives the poem its emotional and psychological impact, impact which would be weakened or lacking in mere battles with other men. Read as the story of a man battling the forces of darkness, the poem has extraordinary power, and an inherent sadness which makes it immensely moving. It is not an epic, says Tolkien; it is an elegy, lament and praise for a man who died as all men must, fighting "that battle with the hostile world and the offspring of the dark which ends for all, even the kings and champions, in defeat." For Tolkien the point of the poem is the beauty and glory of such a battle, made more beautiful and more glorious precisely because its inevitable end is death.

The essay is grounded in Tolkien's comprehensive knowledge of Old English and of the early medieval period, but he transcends scholarship to *enter into* the mood and theme of the poem with an intuitive sympathy few scholars

---

*I except folklorists and anthropologists such as Propp, Thompson, and Aarne, whose interest in and study of folk and fairy tales is oriented more toward analysis of motifs and folklore elements than toward appreciation of the tales as literature.

trouble to muster. His review and refutation of the criticism ends not with a summation of the state of the question, but with a vivid and moving allegory, one of the few he ever wrote:

> A man inherited a field in which was an accumulation of old stone, part of an older hall. Of the old stone some had already been used in building the house in which he actually lived, not far from the old house of his fathers. Of the rest he took some and built a tower. But his friends coming perceived at once (without troubling to climb the steps) that these stones had formerly belonged to a more ancient building. So they pushed the tower over, with no little labour, in order to look for hidden carvings and inscriptions, or to discover whence the man's distant forefathers had obtained their building material. . . . And even the man's own descendants, who might have been expected to consider what he had been about, were heard to murmur: 'He is such an odd fellow! Imagine his using these old stones just to build a nonsensical tower! Why did he not restore the old house? He had no sense of proportion.' But from the top of that tower the man had been able to look out upon the sea. (BMC, pp. 54-55)

The allegory is straightforward, and the concept behind it is particularly suited to Tolkien's approach to language. The old stone is the myth-infused Old English language, and anyone familiar with Old English will recognize the aptness of the image. Old English is a massive-sounding language; the words have weight. They are great blocks of sound, craggy-edged and dense with meaning. Language as building-blocks—a concept underlying the word/percept correlation on which Tolkien's myth is founded—finds mention later in the essay, where Tolkien compares the balance of the Old English poetic line to masonry (BMC, p. 83). The older hall from which the stones are taken is the ancient heritage of myth, legend, and history, which informs the poet's diction, the word-hoard which is the poet's stock in trade. The house in which he actually lived, for which some of the old stones had been used, would be the living language as the poet spoke it. And the tower is, of course, the poem, the monumental work of art.

The image of the sea is the least specific in the allegory, and for this reason may convey the greatest wealth of meaning. One purpose of the tower—the poem—is to afford a view of the sea, but Tolkien leaves open what may be contained in that view, or what may be its value to the viewer. In myth and psychology the sea is often a representation of the unconscious, or uncontrollable forces, or of death and birth. But Tolkien need not have made deliberate use of such archetypes for the image to be evocative. At its most literal, the image of the sea conveys a sense of limitlessness, a vastness beckoning beyond the confines of ordinary life. The power of the sea has been acknowledged and invoked by writers from the "Seafarer" poet to Melville and Arnold. Tolkien's reference to *garsecg*, the shoreless sea, clearly plays on the idea of the limitless, perhaps the infinite.

The allegory's final image combining sea and tower will be familiar to anyone who has read *The Lord of the Rings*, where the same combination occurs in an oddly evocative episode wholly unconnected with the plot. Asleep and dreaming in the house at Crickhollow, Frodo hears what he at first takes to be wind in the trees, but then realizes is the sound of the sea, "a sound he had never heard in waking life, though it had often troubled his dreams."[3] Finding himself on an open heath, he sees "a tall white tower standing alone on a high ridge. A great desire came over him to climb the tower and see the Sea" (*LOTR*, I, p. 154). In this passage both sea and tower are actual rather than metaphoric, and both have great significance in the previous history of The Silmarillion, but the reader does not need to know this in order for the passage to be effective. The scene clearly invites comparison with the final line of the allegory in the *Beowulf* essay. In both instances the effect comes less from the images

---

[3] J.R.R. Tolkien, *The Lord of the Rings*, 3 vols. (New York: Ballantine Books, 1965), p. 154. Hereafter page references will be cited parenthetically in the text, with this abbreviation: *LOTR*.

of sea and tower than from the stated or implied desire to climb up and look outward to the immense unknown. Tolkien's use of this idea in both the essay and *The Lord of the Rings* suggests that for him it transcended allegory to express an indefinable but very real attribute of the human psyche: the desire to seek something without knowing what it is.

In the context of the essay, those who will not climb the tower, but instead push it over in order to exercise their scholarship, deny this attribute. They will not give themselves to the structure and purpose of the poem, and so have no opportunity to be carried beyond themselves. More than that, they ignore the possibility that this can happen and negate any poetic vision by their stubborn search through the tumbled stones for the non-poetic—those hidden carvings or inscriptions which, in the allegory, stand for purely historical or sociological information. They have no sympathy with the tower's proper use, which is to provide a vision of the sea.

It is particularly important to Tolkien's allegory, and perhaps to an understanding of how he reads *Beowulf*, that the view from the tower leads the eye outward, not upward. The vision carries no promise of hope or salvation. Tolkien has pictured man as living "beneath the sky's inaccessible roof," a phrase which gives the idea of sky as ceiling, a limit on the upward reach of human speculation. He may have felt that a culture which made no distinction between sky and clouds, but used the same word—*wolcen**—for both, would not be likely to find infinity by looking up.

The effect of the poem comes from an understanding of the inevitability of the hero's defeat. The poet has taken care that there should be no suspense whatever about the out-

---

*This may simply be a comment on English weather, but it invites inquiry into the nature of Anglo-Saxon perception. *Wolcen* is most often translated as "cloud" in compounds such as *wolcen-faru*, "cloud host," and *wolcen-wyrcende*, "cloud-producing." See Joseph Bosworth, *An Anglo-Saxon Dictionary*, edited and enlarged by T. Northcote Toller (Oxford: Clarendon Press, 1898), pp. 1263-1264, and John R. Clark Hall, *A Concise Anglo-Saxon Dictionary*, 3rd ed., revised and enlarged (Cambridge: Cambridge University Press, 1931), p. 418.

come. Beowulf, like all heroes and indeed all men, is going to die. *"He is a man,"* says Tolkien, *"and that for him and for many is sufficient tragedy."* A stark statement, and he follows it with one even more bleak: *"lif is læne: eal scæceð leoht and lif somod* [life is transitory*: light and life together hasten away]" (BMC, p. 68). Light, like man, is perishable, finally to be overcome by the dark. The heroes, those "mighty men upon earth" with courage (not hope nor faith) as their stay, must leave the precarious little circle of light to go out into darkness, to battle with darkness—and to lose. This heroism in the face of inevitable defeat is the point of the poem, the pinnacle of the tower which affords the view. Tolkien says of it: "It glimpses the cosmic [the sea, perhaps?] and moves with the thought of all men concerning the fate of human life and efforts" (BMC, p. 87).

It is not *just* death, according to Tolkien, that gives *Beowulf* its meaning and its theme, but death by the forces of darkness which are the monsters. "It is just because the main foes in *Beowulf* are inhuman that the story is larger and more significant," he says (BMC, p. 87). The glory of the doomed battle lies as much in the nature of the opponent as in the fatality of the outcome. No mere struggle against another man would carry this weight of meaning. Beowulf must fight monsters—things frighteningly larger and other than himself—for his defeat to be so overwhelming, his death so grand, that by means of it the reader can glimpse the shoreless sea.

For all his praise of the poem's quality of pagan stoicism, Tolkien sees the *Beowulf* poet as a Christian writing about a pagan past, a not-too-distant past which still held his imagination. "The shadow of its despair, if only as a mood, as an intense emotion of regret, is still there" (BMC, p. 73). That Tolkien is in sympathy with this despair is clear, but it is also clear that for him this in no way contradicts Christianity, "For the monsters do not depart, whether the gods go or come. A Christian was (and is) still like his forefathers a mortal hemmed in a hostile world" (BMC, p. 72). While the

---

*Literally *loaned*.

poem may have been written, as Tolkien suggests, at the point of intersection between new Christianity and old pagan tradition, its author, however Christian he may have been, "is still concerned with *man on earth*, rehandling in a new perspective an ancient theme: that man, each man and all men and all their works shall die. A theme no Christian need despise" (BMC, p. 73).

The phrase *"man on earth,"* emphasized by the italics, is the key to Tolkien's reading of the meeting of paganism and Christianity in the poem, and in his own philosophy as well. Humankind lives in a fallen world, a hostile environment within which man will surely die. Beowulf stands for all men as much as for all heroes, "fallen and not yet saved, disgraced but not dethroned" (BMC, p. 74). His battle is that of all mortal men, and that battle and the defeat which follows it constitute a theme which no Christian, including Tolkien in his own work, need despise.

For all his understanding of the *Beowulf* poet's use of monsters, Tolkien brings to the subject the perspective of his own century, as well as an understanding of the Middle Ages. His defense of the monsters is psychological rather than allegorical. Grendel and the dragon are both monsters, true, but they are not the same *kind* of monster, and in distinguishing between them Tolkien is a modern, however great his pull toward the past. "In a sense," he says in a note, "the foe is always both within and without. ... Thus Grendel has a perverted human shape. ... For it is true of man, maker of myths, that Grendel and the Dragon, in their lust, greed, and malice, have a part in him" (BMC, p. 76). The monsters are within us as well as outside us. The hostile dark is a part of man, not just his besieging foe. The dragon may be the instrument of final defeat, but Grendel carries his own kind of threat to humanity, for he moves in the shape of a man. And though the youthful Beowulf is victorious in his struggle with Grendel, that inner darkness, no less than the dragon's, is always there to be battled.

The recurrence of these references to darkness, to the precariousness of the light, to the monsters, is forceful evidence of the emotional pull of the dark for Tolkien. His own reading of Christianity tends to emphasize the tragedy of the Fall and its consequences. His ability to enter into the mood and spirit of the poem suggests strongly that he knew the subject firsthand, and that he had found out, as Humphrey Carpenter said, that no battle would be won forever. He could not have such an intensely sympathetic approach to the poem if it did not strike a chord in his own nature. It seems clear that however he may qualify the pagan point of view, his heart is with the tragedy.

To turn from the *Beowulf* essay to "On Fairy-stories" is to turn from dark to light. In attitude and spirit one could not be further from the other. This is, of course, largely a function of the markedly different subject matter; fairy-stories are based on hope, not pessimism, and however terrifying the adventures, they always culminate in the happy ending. But the choice of subject is again an indication of that antithesis so deeply rooted in Tolkien's nature. That he could be so powerfully attracted to such opposing outlooks shows plainly the antinomian tension in his own psychology.

Where the *Beowulf* essay extolled courage, the fairy-story essay values enchantment. The emphasis is on man's need for the beauty and wonder of another world rather than his inevitable defeat in this one. Instead of drawing a circle of light surrounded by darkness, Tolkien calls our attention to what he calls the "perilous realm," the otherworld of Faërie. Both worlds are dangerous, but the dark, northern view is replaced in the fairy-story essay by a greater and brighter danger—danger of losing one's self and finding another and perhaps a higher world.

The essays are different in kind as well as in subject matter. The *Beowulf* essay is a close analysis of a single poem. Although Tolkien draws widely on his knowledge of medieval heroic and religious literature, it is all in the service of bringing out the meaning of the poem. By contrast, the fairy-story essay is broad and less focused. It is an extraordinary amalgam of genre-history, critical analysis, theory of fiction, and critical philosophy. A kind of latter-day defense of poesy, it owes a considerable debt to the Romantics, and particularly to Coleridge. Beyond this, it is a trove of information about Tolkien's thoughts, feelings, and critical reactions to his own work. Interspersed with discussion of the nature of fairy-stories and of the criteria for creating fantasy are phrases and allusions—almost asides—which, read in the context of Tolkien's fiction, become specific references to aspects of his own work. These allusions, always germane to the discussion of the essay, are windows into Tolkien's mind, affording a look at the creative process as well as the critical one.

First delivered at St. Andrews University on March 8, 1939, as the Andrew Lang Lecture for that year, the fairy-story essay came more than two years after the one on *Beowulf* and at a time when Tolkien's thoughts and energies were even more involved with his creative work. *The Hobbit* had just been published, and he was beginning work on "the new Hobbit," which was to become *The Lord of the Rings* and which—in the manner of *Beowulf*—was already reaching backward into that "dark antiquity of sorrow" that is The Silmarillion. It comes as no surprise, therefore, that although the subject of the essay is fairy-stories, a considerable part of it is devoted to the hows and whys of myth and fantasy.

Tolkien opens by asking three questions: "What are fairy-stories? What is their origin? What is the use of them?" (OFS, p. 33). And, as with the *Beowulf* essay, he begins by refuting some commonly-held misapprehensions, in this case that fairies are tiny sprites, and that fairy-stories are stories about fairies. Fairies are creatures of enchantment whatever their size (and diminutive fairies are late arrivals to the genre), and fairy-stories are about human beings who in some way wander into or interact with the enchanted world of Faërie. By "Faërie" Tolkien means fay-er-ie, the quality of enchantment, and this quality above all distinguishes fairy-stories from ordinary stories.

As to their origin, Tolkien concedes that this is a complex question, not susceptible of easy analysis. "To ask what is the origin of stories (however qualified) is to ask what is the origin of language and the mind" (OFS, p. 44). This relationship between mind, language, and story is of especial importance to Tolkien's mythology, for it is the basis of his myth and the genesis of his fiction. "The incarnate mind, the tongue, and the tale are in our world coeval" (OFS, p. 48). Easier to address is the question of what they are now, however they may have originated. Whether they arise from independent invention, or from diffusion (he calls it "borrowing in space"), or from inheritance (which he calls "borrowing in time") is of less concern to him than the nature of the story *as we have it.* Whatever may have been the circumstances of their origin, the stories are all now part of what he calls the Pot of Soup, the Cauldron of Story which has been simmering since imagination first found expression in words. Myth, history, legend, and folktale all are thrown into the Pot at one time or another, and all contribute to the flavor of the Soup. What is ladled out in any given instance is *a story,* and it is the story as we have it to which we respond, not to the raw ingredients as they went into the Pot.

Of his three questions, the third—"What is the use of them?"—is by far the most important in Tolkien's estimation, for it is the effect of a work of imagination that keeps it alive. The effect of *Beowulf* was to give a vision of the shoreless sea, immensity beyond the ordinary world. What is the use, the effect, the value of fairy-stories? Tolkien's answer is even clearer than in the *Beowulf* essay, for it comes directly rather than as allegory. Fairy-stories offer their readers four things that the human spirit needs: Fantasy, Recovery, Escape, and Consolation. Of these, the primary element is Fantasy, for the other three derive from it. Fantasy is both a mode of thinking and the created result of that thinking. Recovery, Escape, and Consolation are experiential terms describing varieties of response to Fantasy.

The section of the essay about Fantasy owes a clear debt to Romantic critical theory, and especially to Coleridge's famous statements on Imagination. But Tolkien is not in complete agreement with Coleridge, and uses the essay to set him straight on one or two points. Where Coleridge distinguishes between Imagination and Fancy, finding them to be different in kind and Imagination much the greater, Tolkien sees them as different only in degree. Coleridge recognizes Primary

Imagination, Secondary Imagination, and Fancy. The Primary Imagination is for him "a repetition in the finite mind of the eternal act of creation in the infinite I Am." This is the manifestation of God's creative Logos—the Word—in the human mind. Secondary Imagination is alike in kind, but lesser in degree. It is an echo of the Primary Imagination "co-existing with the conscious will," more human, less God-like, yet in essence the same. Fancy, on the other hand, is in Coleridge's view only "a mode of memory" with "no other counters to play with but fixities and definites."[4] Fancy has no power to create. It can remember, but it cannot make.

Tolkien disagrees. In his view, Fancy—"image-making"— is different from Imagination only in degree. Imagination is "the power of giving to ideal creations the inner consistency of reality," and Fancy is simply one aspect of this power. "The perception of the image, the grasp of its implications, and the control which are necessary to a successful expression may vary in vividness and strength: but this is a difference of degree in Imagination, not in kind" (OFS, p. 68). *Fancy*, says Tolkien, is simply a reduced form of the older word *Fantasy*. Under the heading of this older word he combines both Fancy and Imagination, together with that art by which they are made manifest, an art he calls sub-creation. The term as Tolkien uses it embraces Coleridge's "repetition in the finite mind of the eternal act of creation." In Tolkien's words, Fantasy "combines with its older and higher use as an equivalent of Imagination the derived notions of 'unreality' (that is, of unlikeness to the Primary World), of freedom from the domination of observed 'fact,' in short of the fantastic" (OFS, p. 69). It is "the making or glimpsing of Other-worlds." Successful Fantasy is the conscious sub-creation of a Secondary

---

[4]This is, of course, from the famous Chapter Thirteen of Samuel Taylor Coleridge's landmark in Romantic criticism, *Biographia Literaria*, of which the definitive edition is the Shawcross (Oxford, 1907). My citation comes from *Criticism: The Major Texts*, ed. W.J. Bate (New York: Harcourt Brace Jovanovich, 1970), p. 387, but these comments by Coleridge are to be found in any anthology of Romantic Criticism.

World by man, whose birthright it is to make in imitation of his Maker.

The other three terms—Recovery, Escape, and Consolation—describe the effects of successful Fantasy on the reader. The first term, Recovery, relates to the principle of the "Chaucer" and "*Sigelwara Land*" essays; it is a getting back of what was originally there. It is a re-gaining of a clear view, "seeing things as we are (or were) meant to see them" (OFS, p. 77). Through Fantasy we recover a fresh view of the unfantastic, a view too often dulled by long familiarity. The fantastic should help us to see the ordinary as if for the first time, to regain a sense of its extraordinariness. "We should look at green again, and be startled anew (but not blinded) by blue and yellow and red. We should see the centaur and the dragon, and then perhaps suddenly behold, like the ancient shepherds, sheep, and dogs, and horses—and wolves. This recovery fairy-stories help us to make" (OFS, p. 77). As Tolkien describes it, his concept of Recovery is not unlike the Platonic concept of recollection, the idea—best expressed in the *Timaeus*—that knowledge is recollection of things already learned, that we constantly re-discover and re-possess what we have formerly known.

Sub-creation thus has a purpose beyond itself. The making of a Secondary World is not simply to produce enchantment as its end result. The Secondary World should re-direct our attention to the Primary World, and through that to its Maker, should enable us to re-gain, to re-collect what we have known but have forgotten how to look at. Through imitation of God man has the opportunity to recover Him.

Tolkien's other terms—Escape and Consolation—are closely connected, for it is through escape that we experience consolation. But the word *escape* must itself be recovered and re-explored in order to fully appreciate Tolkien's use of the word. "Escapist" literature is generally thought of as diversionary reading, a temporary distraction from the often unpleasant facts of "real" life. Tolkien does not argue with this view, but he does defend the motive behind it, finding "escapism" to be valid. He has little use for "real" life if the reality includes the grim face of industrialism, urban blight, and the noise of traffic and machinery. If escape can take us away from these things into a world more beautiful (if no less terrible), then escape is a good thing. The march of technology, with all its contributions to modern life, serves largely to make things obsolete so that they may be replaced with ever newer things, fated to be replaced in their turn. For Tolkien, the beauties and eternalities of myth and Faërie, un-"real" though they may seem, have outlasted and will outlast the artifacts and improvements of ever-changing technology.

A strong reactionary feeling is evident here, which did much to shape and color Tolkien's Middle-earth. He finds many of the developments of modern life to be ugly and destructive in effect, whatever may be their intent. His notion of escape is informed by longing for a simpler world like that of his childhood, a world which was fast disappearing even then. And so nostalgia for time past permeates the melancholy gold-and-silver beauty of Lórien, the pastoral quiet of the Shire, even the wilderness of Fangorn Forest. Counterpoised to these are the belching furnaces, reeking smoke, sooty chimneys, and war machinery of Saruman and Mordor, and the corruption of the Shire.

But this is more than mere reaction, more than nostalgia; it is only one aspect of an infinitely older and more profound longing which Tolkien suggests fantasy can satisfy, if only for a while. For, he says, "there are ancient limitations from which fairy-stories offer a sort of escape, and old ambitions and desires (touching the very roots of fantasy) to which they offer a kind of satisfaction and consolation" (OFS, p. 83). Some are simple, "such as the desire to visit, free as a fish, the deep sea; or the longing . . . for the flight of a bird." Others are more profound, such as "the desire to converse with other living things. On this desire, as ancient as the Fall, is largely founded the talking of beasts and creatures in fairy-tales, and especially the magical understanding of their proper speech" (OFS, p. 84).

The phrase "as ancient as the Fall" is the key to the underlying concern in this part of Tolkien's discussion. Here he has gone beyond that simple nostalgia for the past and for childhood which he, and all men, have felt at one time or another, to touch what he clearly feels is the deep source of that nostalgia—mankind's longing for its own past, the childhood before the Fall. As he sees it, then, the need for escape arises more from the desire to return than from the need to get away. The magical speech of beasts in fairy tales is to Tolkien a symptom of our sense of separation and our longing for re-union. "A vivid sense of that separation is ancient," he says; and the repetition of "ancient" connects separation with Fall. But he goes even further, to say that we have also "a sense that it was a severance; a strange fate and a guilt lie on us" (OFS, p. 84). "Severance" is a harsher term than "separation," suggesting a sharp cutting-off of things once rightly joined. His use in the next phrase of the word "guilt" connects the blame for this to mankind. Clearly the discussion here is more theological than literary. Tolkien's juxtaposition of "separation," "severance," and "guilt" with the Fall gives all three words a greater yet more specific meaning than the ordinary. Separation—no, *severance*—is the Fall, severance from God and from the rest of creation, the original sin from which all the others come.

Beyond the satisfaction (if only for a little while) of these primal, ancient desires is the ability of the fairy-story to give its readers what Tolkien calls the Consolation of the Happy Ending. This last concept Tolkien finds so important that he has coined a new term for the moment in the story which leads to that ending: *eucatastrophe.* With that return to literal meaning which is a Tolkien trademark, he has carefully built the term on its earliest use and from its earliest components. *Katastrophe* is the dénouement of classical Greek tragedy, coming from *katastrephein,* "to turn down or overturn."[5] Tolkien's addition of *eu,* "well or good," reverses the

---

[5]All definitions and etymologies are taken from *The American Heritage Dictionary,* ed. William Morris (New York: American Heritage Publishing Company, 1970). The Indo-European root is cited at the end of the word-entry, and refers the reader to the Appendix on "Indo-European Roots," done by Calvert Watkins of the Department of Linguistics, Harvard University. Watkins' entries refer the reader to the final authority in the field, Julius Pokorny's *Indogermanisches Etymologisches Wörterbuch* (Bern: Francke Verlag, 1959), but Watkins differs from Pokorny in some instances.

tragic meaning to turn the word into "the good overturning," the moment in the fairy tale when evil is overthrown and good triumphs.

This is the "good catastrophe" referred to in the earlier citation from the essay, the "sudden joyous 'turn' " of events when we know past all hope that everything is going to be all right. Tolkien makes clear, however, that the consolation of this moment is dependent on the likelihood that it will not happen, that instead there will be *dyscatastrophe*, sorrow, and failure. This ever-present possibility is what makes the joy at deliverance so piercing, and leads to the denial of "universal final defeat." This is the moment in the fairy tale when the kiss awakes the sleeping princess, when the slipper fits the little foot, when Beauty's declaration of love resurrects and transforms the dying Beast.

So closely is this Consolation tied to the last escape on Tolkien's list that one cannot properly be considered without the other. The last escape he calls "the Great Escape: the Escape from Death" (OFS, p. 85). The desire to escape from death is one which concerns Tolkien deeply. He wrote of *The Lord of the Rings*, "It is mainly concerned with Death, and Immortality" (*TLOT*, p. 284), and the same concern is evident in *The Silmarillion*. Through immortal elves and mortal men Tolkien explores the positive and negative sides of death, of its opposite—unending life—and of its corollary—life eternal. He makes a clear distinction between unending life, which he sees as bondage to the world without hope of renewal, and eternal life, which transcends death and leads to God. As Tolkien points out, fairy-stories are written by men, not fairies. They are concerned with the escape from death, whereas "the Human-stories of the elves are doubtless full of the escape from deathlessness" (OFS, p. 85). Each wants what the other has without understanding what it is. For deathlessness is not true immortality; it is simply prolongation of life. The real escape from death is *through* death to eternal life. The final Consolation, the Great Escape, denies "universal final defeat" because it shows the reader life beyond death. This is Tolkien's *evangelium*, "giving a fleeting glimpse of Joy . . . beyond the walls of the world, poignant as grief."

As with *eucatastrophe*, Tolkien chooses *evangelium* and

joy for their earliest and most literal meaning. *Evangelium* is Late Latin "good news," for which the Old English translation is *godspell*, which becomes *gospel*, and thus a major part of the Christian *mythos*. And when we find that *joy* comes from Latin *gaudére*, "to rejoice," and can be traced back to Indo-European *gáu-*, "to rejoice, *to have religious fear or awe*" (italics mine), the direction of Tolkien's thinking becomes clear.

His epilogue to the essay makes it plain, for here he connects the fairy-story directly to the Christian Gospels. In Tolkien's eyes, the Gospels contain "a fairy-story, or a story of a larger kind which embraces all the essence of fairy-stories" (OFS, p. 88). This is true *evangelium*, good news, which imparts joy—both rejoicing and religious awe. Certainly this is "Joy beyond the walls of the world," for, says Tolkien, "this story has entered History and the primary world; the desire and aspiration of sub-creation have been raised to the fulfillment of creation. The birth of Christ is the eucatastrophe of Man's history. The Resurrection is the eucatastrophe of the story of the Incarnation" (OFS, pp. 88-89).

Tolkien is in good critical company here. Erich Auerbach points out in *Mimesis*, his discussion of the representation of reality in Western literature, that the story of Christ is such an integral part of the mind and imagination of Western man that it has informed almost all Western narrative since its time, and has made the mix of everyday reality and high tragedy the norm for narrative literature.[6] Tolkien goes a step further. For him this mixture—potential tragedy and the happy ending, operating as reality within history—embraces the form of the fairy tale while lifting the reader beyond that secondary belief demanded by fiction to the level of primary belief in the Primary World.

For Tolkien the Christian story is the greatest fairy-story of all because it is not fiction but fact. This story comes not from man's imagination (though it has the power to inspire

---

[6]Erich Auerbach, *Mimesis*, trans. Willard B. Trask (Princeton: Princeton University Press, 1953).

it), but from recorded history. It has bridged the gap between Primary and Secondary Worlds, and fulfilled in Creation mankind's longing for both Escape and Consolation. And this is Consolation of the highest kind, absolving guilt, promising re-union, looking forward to the final Happy Ending.

In doing this for man it has of necessity changed him. The turn in the fairy-story is the reversal of direction when the downward trend swings suddenly upward. To read of the turn is to experience it, to undergo a change of mood from dark to light, from despair to joy. This is *metanoia*, reversal of the direction of the mind. The same word means "repentance." The turn, then, is a kind of conversion, and what we feel at the turn in a fairy-story is, to however small a degree, a conversion experience. In Tolkien's terms it would be a Secondary experience, echoing what is for him the Primary experience at the turn of the Christian story, the Resurrection. This would have, he says, "exactly the same quality, if not the same degree, as the joy which the 'turn' in a fairy-story gives: such joy has the very taste of primary truth. (Otherwise its name would not be joy.)" (OFS, p. 89). At this point all four of Tolkien's terms—Fantasy, Recovery, Escape, Consolation—come together to demonstrate what Tolkien finds in fairy-stories, and what he wants all readers to find.

The two essays, with their complex messages of glory in defeat and *dyscatastrophe* as the necessary prelude to *eucatastrophe*, are the hallmarks of a complex man, and are the keys to his mythology. Both essays acknowledge and affirm the necessity of dark and light in man's world. Tolkien sees the *Beowulf* poet as a Christian, a man "looking back into the pit . . . perceiving [the] common tragedy of inevitable ruin, and yet feeling this more *poetically* because he was himself removed from the direct pressure of its despair" (BMC, p. 73). Tolkien, too, is writing as a Christian, for all that the impact of his essay comes from his knowledge of the power of darkness. He can, and does, feel "the direct pressure of despair"; otherwise he could not write so movingly about it. But his faith resists this pressure with its affirmation of the doctrine of salvation. "Man on earth" is doomed to defeat, as the essay makes clear, but that is only as far as man can see. There is hope beyond the earth.

In *Beowulf* and in Tolkien's essay about the poem the hope is only a hope, not an observable reality. But in the fairy-story essay that hope is validated by the historicity of Christ and the observable Happy Ending of the Resurrection. Still, that does not mean there is no darkness. If the outcome of the story is not truly in doubt, always in doubt, there can be no turn. The doubt must be real; it must come from knowledge that there may be no happy ending, that the thing which we greatly fear may come upon us.

And so doubt cannot be dismissed too easily or too quickly. It is a functional element necessary to the tone of both essays, stemming from the outlook of their author. Indeed, doubt is the starting-point for the epilogue of the fairy-story essay. Tolkien says of the story of Christ: "There is no tale ever told that men would rather find was true, and none which so many sceptical men have accepted as true on its own merits. . . . To reject it leads either to sadness or to wrath" (OFS, p. 89). Certainly Tolkien did not reject it.

But the phrase "would rather" is curiously cautious, cast in the subjunctive mood rather than the indicative. It describes what men want, not what men know. I do not mean to suggest that Tolkien did not think the story was true. Nothing in his life is clearer than his commitment to Christianity. And it is important to remember that he is speaking in the context of stories that are not true—that is, fairy-stories. A few lines further on in the essay he declares straight out: "This story is supreme; and it is true" (OFS, p. 89). This is in the indicative mood; it has the ring of conviction. Yet his prior words somewhat rob the statement of its force. Hope, doubt, and certainty are mingled.

There is precedent for Tolkien in the outcry on the Cross. If Christ felt forsaken, however briefly, surely doubt is admissible in his followers. The moment of greatest separation from God is also the moment of greatest awareness of him. Faith needs doubt as up needs down and light needs dark— to define by opposition. The ability to acknowledge contradictory concepts and to hold them in balanced tension is a hallmark of the creative mind. Quite clearly it is a hallmark of Tolkien's mind, central to his philosophy and his fiction. In the work, as in the man, doubt and affirmation, despair and hope are positive and negative poles, creating the force field which generates his Secondary World. The polarities of light and dark give rise to the perception, the language, and thus the action of The Silmarillion.

III
Poetic Diction and Splintered Light

Mythology is the ghost of concrete meaning.

OWEN BARFIELD, POETIC DICTION

Both the Secondary World and the force field which holds it are built up out of words. Tolkien's response to words, to their shape and sound and meaning, was instinctive, intuitive as well as intellectual, so that he approached words more as a musician than as a grammarian. His life-long occupation with the history of words came to maturity during a time of philological and linguistic ferment of which he was very much a part. The early years of the twentieth century were a time when philology, mythology, and anthropology were coming to be seen as formed from the same matrix. Work done in all these fields seemed to be overlapping significantly and producing a far more sophisticated and cohesive picture of ancient cultures than that painted by the nineteenth century. In particular, work done by Owen Barfield in England and Ernst Cassirer in Germany suggested an interconnectedness of myth and language which spoke directly to Tolkien's interests, both professional and avocational. Of the two men, Barfield seems to have been the stronger influence on Tolkien; while he could have made use of Cassirer's books, they were not available in English translation until much later.

Sometime in 1928 Tolkien's friend and Oxford colleague C.S. Lewis remarked to Barfield, a longtime friend: "You might like to know that when Tolkien dined with me the other night he said, *à propos* of something quite different, that your conception of the ancient semantic unity had modified his whole outlook, and that he was always just going to say something in a lecture when your concept stopped him in time. 'It is one of those things,' he said, 'that when you've once seen it there are all sorts of things you can never say again.' "[1]

The conception of ancient semantic unity to which Tolkien alluded is the central thesis of one of Barfield's most important critical books, *Poetic Diction*, published in 1928 and, quite clearly, freshly read by Tolkien. His comment that Barfield's book had modified his whole outlook is sweeping, and invites investigation. Given Tolkien's life-long fascination with words and myth, his near-encyclopedic knowledge of languages, their history and the principles underlying their formation and modification, what sort of concept could be persuasive enough to modify his whole outlook? A very simple one, as it turns out, but one—like so many simple things—with profound philosophical implications. Some knowledge of Barfield's theory, therefore, its development and its ramifications, will throw valuable light on Tolkien's attitude toward language and his use of it to create his mythology.

Barfield is a difficult man to categorize because his interests extend over a wide range of disciplines. By profession he was for many years a solicitor. By avocation and natural inclination he is a philologist, a mythologist, and perhaps most seriously a philosopher, since his work in this area encompasses the other two and draws extensively on his accumulated knowledge of those fields.

Because of shared interests, and even more because of his friendship with C.S. Lewis, Barfield was a member (now one of the last surviving) of that informal discussion group which called itself the Inklings, and gathered in Lewis's rooms at Oxford to drink and talk and read aloud from works in progress. From all accounts Barfield and Tolkien enjoyed one another's company, but they were both better friends with Lewis than with one another. Barfield had known Lewis since they were both undergraduates at Oxford, and their friendship continued and deepened during annual walking-tours of England, stimulated by a running battle of ideas which they called "The Great War." This lively debate pitted Lewis's then-agnostic rationalism against Barfield's conviction, based on his

---

[1]Humphrey Carpenter, *The Inklings* (Boston: Houghton Mifflin, 1979), p. 51.

reading of Rudolf Steiner, that imagination can be used quite as well as logic and reason to gain a better understanding of phenomena and to comprehend the world around us.

Barfield's reading of Steiner had led him to adopt Steiner's religious philosophy, called Anthroposophy. It is a difficult philosophy to synopsize, or to briefly explain and describe. Indeed, Barfield has said that he spent an evening explaining Anthroposophy to the Inklings at their request, and found it a formidable task.[2] Humphrey Carpenter gives a cogent, brief account of Anthroposophy in his discussion of Barfield in *The Inklings,* his companion volume to the Tolkien biography. Some account is necessary here for a proper understanding of Barfield's own writing.

Steiner's philosophy, which he felt was fundamentally Christian though not sectarian, holds that the process of evolution, which involves not only mankind but the whole universe, is anthropocentric, and is a process of coming to consciousness in which man has become progressively more aware of himself and his surroundings, while at the same time becoming increasingly separate from the world around him and from the power which began the whole process. This coming to consciousness, now at a stage in which man is completely separated from the natural and the supernatural world, is a necessary step in the progression to full consciousness, in which man will be at once fully aware of himself as an individual and fully aware of his union with God and the universe.

While they apparently found Anthroposophy a bit hard to grasp, the Inklings had much in common with Barfield in other and related areas. All were staunch Christians, and all were interested in myth, in words, in fantasy, in literature. Tolkien was a regular participant in Inkling gatherings; Barfield was, as he puts it, "really only on the fringe."[3] He could not be a regular, since the group was largely a part of the

---

[2]Letter from Owen Barfield to the author, October 9, 1980.

[3]Shirley Sugerman, "A Conversation with Owen Barfield," in *Evolution of Consciousness: Studies in Polarity,* ed. Shirley Sugerman (Middletown, Conn.: Wesleyan University Press, 1977), p. 10.

Oxford community and his home and his work were in London. Nevertheless, though Barfield attended the meetings infrequently, he and Tolkien had some important interests and attitudes in common, and clearly found places where their minds touched. In particular, they shared an abiding interest in the history of language and its relationship to mythology. Beyond these mutual interests they seem to have shared a certain community of mind, for Barfield has said that in some areas, most notably in the concept of the poet as world-maker ("sub-creator" is Tolkien's term), he felt that Tolkien was rather closer to his own point of view than was Lewis, with whom Barfield enjoyed not so much community of mind as vigorous and challenging interaction.[4]

Certainly Barfield's published work, particularly his early books, reflects many of the same interests which occupied Tolkien. When he wrote *Poetic Diction*, Barfield was already the author of a number of articles and reviews, a children's book called *The Silver Trumpet*, and a book on the history of language, *History in English Words*. The genesis of *Poetic Diction* was an article which Barfield had written in 1922 on the history and changing meaning of the word *ruin*. By 1928 this article was one chapter in the larger, more comprehensive *Poetic Diction*, sub-titled *A Study in Meaning*. The focus had expanded from considering the changes in one word to exploring the whole question of meaning, and of the relation of perception to word and word to concept. It became, in Barfield's words, "not merely a theory of poetic diction, but a theory of poetry; and not merely a theory of poetry, but a theory of knowledge."[5] While the theory itself is simple and straightforward, it has profound implications for the development of language and perception, and the interrelationship of phenomenon, word, and meaning. It does not lend itself

---

[4]Owen Barfield to the author during a conversation at Barfield's home, Kent, England, May 28, 1981.

[5]Owen Barfield, *Poetic Diction: A Study in Meaning*, 3rd ed. (Middletown, Conn.: Wesleyan University Press, 1973), p. 14. Hereafter page references will be cited parenthetically in the text, with this abbreviation: *PD*.

well to paraphrase; Barfield's argument is so tightly constructed that all parts are interdependent and equally important in their support of the thesis. Nevertheless, some
explanation is necessary to develop an understanding of Tolkien's ready acceptance of the theory and a grasp of his use
of it in his own work.

Barfield suggests that myth, language, and man's perception of his world are inseparable. Words are expressed myth,
the embodiment of mythic concepts and a mythic world view.
The word *myth*, in this context, must be taken to mean that
which describes man's perception of his relationship to the
natural and supernatural world. Barfield's theory postulates
that language, in its beginnings, made no distinction between
the literal and the metaphoric meaning of a word, as it does
today. Indeed, the very concept of metaphor, of one thing
described in terms of another, was non-existent. All diction
was literal, directly giving voice to man's perception of phenomena and his intuitive mythic participation in them. The
modern distinction between the literal and the metaphoric
use of a word suggests a separation of the abstract from the
concrete which did not exist in earlier times. Man in his
beginnings had a vision of the cosmos as a whole, and of
himself as a part of it, a vision which he has long since left
behind. We now perceive the cosmos as particularized, fragmented, and wholly separate from ourselves. Our consciousness and the language with which we express it have changed
and splintered. In that earlier, primal world-view, every word
would have had its own unified meaning, embodying what
we now can understand only as a multiplicity of concepts,
concepts for which we (no longer able to participate in the
original world and world view) must use many different words.

For example, the Greek *pneuma* and the Latin *spiritus*
each expressed a concept in which "wind," "breath," and
"spirit" were all perceived as the same phenomenon. Barfield
notes that in the third chapter of the New Testament Gospel
according to Saint John the word *pneuma* is rendered into
English as *spirit* in verse five and as *wind* in verse eight.
Apparently for Saint John and his audience *pneuma* had an
undivided meaning which later perception can no longer grasp

whole, and for which a later mentality must find different words to fit what it perceives as different meanings.

Barfield pushes the concept even further to postulate a kind of proto-meaning antedating even that undivided meaning which we can recognize as lost. He says:

> We must, therefore, imagine a time in which [*pneuma* and *spiritus*], or older words from which these had descended, meant neither *breath*, nor *wind*, nor *spirit*, nor yet all three of these things, but when they simply had *their own old peculiar meaning*, which has since, in the course of the evolution of consciousness, crystallized into the three meanings specified—and no doubt into others also, for which separate words had already been found by Greek and Roman times. (*PD*, p. 81)

The Gospel of Saint John provides another example. In the King James version the opening sentence, "In the Beginning was the Word," gives *word* as the translation for the Greek *logos*. To Saint John and his audience, *logos* would have conveyed—co-equally with *word*—"speech," "reason," "organizing principle," and "cosmic harmony"; all of these concepts would have been apprehended as the same phenomenon. To translate such a word, as we are forced to do today, by selecting any *one* of these meanings is to arbitrarily separate the word from that cluster of concepts which it was meant to express. Word, concept, and percept have altered so that the ancient semantic unity has, of necessity, been fragmented.

Although over-compressed, this summary gives a general idea of the salient features of Barfield's theory, which views words as indices and instruments of developing consciousness. Man's growing consciousness of himself as separate from phenomena, and of various phenomena as discrete from one another, carries with it a consequent fragmentation of perception and vocabulary. As the process continues, this fragmentation of vocabulary itself leads to further fragmentation of perception—more percepts lead to more words which give rise to other percepts which generate new words—and thus a self-perpetuating process is established.

This is the theory which Tolkien told Lewis had "modified his whole outlook." Nor is it difficult to see why. To accept such a theory—and Tolkien clearly did—would be to accept a whole new way of looking at words, to see them not just as parts of a language but as fragments of the Logos and integral elements in man's way of relating to his surroundings. Tolkien commented to Lewis that Barfield's concept "stopped him in time" from saying things about language which he must have then seen as wrong or misleading. This is the negative side of the revelation; but the positive side, far from stopping him from saying things, may have enabled him to say new things. Some evidence for this can be found in "*Sigelwara Land*," which Tolkien wrote some six years after his reading of Barfield; in this essay he finds in the word a way into the perception and imagination of those who used it. Barfield's concept could not have affected Tolkien's philological and scholarly outlook without at the same time coloring his creative work, so much of which was built on and of language. Knowledge, after all, cannot be kept in compartments, but must inevitably spill over from one area into another. When two areas are next door to each other, as was the case with Tolkien's studies and his imaginative fiction, the spill-over is not only inevitable but fruitful, each discipline fructifying the other. Thus Tolkien's fiction enhanced his capacity to imaginatively enter into a culture and its language; his scholarship gave him a solid base on which to imagine peoples and their languages.

The impact of Barfield's concept on Tolkien's thinking is clearly evident in "On Fairy-stories," in which Tolkien is chiefly concerned with the nature of fantasy and the power of language to create a fantasy world. This same attitude toward words is at the heart of the concept which lies behind The Silmarillion, a work of fantasy which strikingly illustrates the very kind of development and fragmentation of language and perception which Barfield's theory describes.

Tolkien began work on his mythology in 1917. Since he was still working and re-working the material at the time of his death more than fifty years later, it seems reasonable to suppose that the tale grew in the telling, and the material expanded and deepened as Tolkien's learning, experience, and knowledge of his craft grew. While his mythology was in the making, his professional work in philology and his study and teaching of early languages and literature continued and developed. His encounter with Barfield's theory in *Poetic Diction* enlarged and deepened his thinking about language. Given the two men's mutual interest in mythology, it may very well have reinforced Tolkien's mythological bent, giving his attitude toward language a more mythical, perhaps more philosophical slant.

Much of this attitude, and much of Tolkien's thinking about his own creative work, is evident in the discussion of language that forms such an important part of the fairy-story essay, which Tolkien composed while he was in the process of writing *The Lord of the Rings* and blending it into his already-created mythological world. Sub-creation, his term for the making of a fantasy world, was the process through which he made The Silmarillion, and the primary tool of his sub-creation was language which he saw and used as Barfield had described it in *Poetic Diction.*

In a rather circular pattern Tolkien's mythology is both a source for and an illustration of the essay. Tolkien lifts the central image from the story—the light—and uses it to express a concept of creative writing. This concept, in turn, describes The Silmarillion in its major aspects of plot and theme. Moreover, these aspects illustrate in concrete terms Tolkien's ideas, developed from Barfield, about the nature and function of language. And, finally, they become the paradigm of his vision of the role and the importance of the fantasy writer.

The critical nexus of the essay is the section in which Tolkien discusses the writing of fantasy as an act of sub-creation. He describes it as the making of a Secondary World in imitation of God, the maker of the Primary World. God is the Prime Mover, the First Creator; man must therefore be a secondary creator, or sub-creator. But for Tolkien this is a high calling; to be second best to God is no mean accomplishment. The tools of sub-creation are words (a sub-genre of the *logos* of Saint John, and thus also in imitation of God).

This being the case, words are not merely for describing or reporting, but for actual making, for realizing (in the literal sense of the word) an imaginary world. Two passages in the essay address this subject, and the similarities and differences between them are revealing. The first deals directly with the word and the power of the word:

> The human mind, endowed with powers of generalization and abstraction, sees not only green-grass, discriminating it from other things (and finding it fair to look upon) but sees that it is *green* as well as being *grass.* But how powerful, how stimulating to the very faculty that produced it, was the invention of the adjective: no spell or incantation in Faërie is more potent. And that is not surprising: such incantations might be said to be only another view of adjectives, a part of speech in a mythical grammar. The mind that thought of *light, heavy, grey, yellow, still, swift,* also conceived of magic that would make heavy things light and able to fly, turn grey lead into yellow gold, and the still rock into a swift water. If it could do the one, it could do the other; it inevitably did both. When we can take green from grass, blue from heaven, and red from blood, we have already an enchanter's power—upon one plane; and the desire to wield that power in the world external to our minds awakes. ... In such "fantasy" as it is called, new form is made; Faërie begins. Man becomes a sub-creator. (OFS, pp. 48-49)

Tolkien's own enchantment with the power of words imbues this passage with vitality and excitement, so that the idea is vividly and energetically conveyed. Nevertheless, he re-works the same idea a few pages later, and in different terms.

The second passage quotes lines from "Mythopoeia," a poem Tolkien wrote in reply to C.S. Lewis, who had argued that myths and fairy tales are *merely* fantasies, lies breathed, as Lewis put it, "through silver." Tolkien's introduction of his poem into the discussion of fantasy and sub-creation in the essay suggests a desire to expand, re-state, perhaps re-define his notion of the process of sub-creation.

"Dear Sir," I said—"Although now long estranged,
Man is not wholly lost nor wholly changed.
Dis-graced he may be, yet is not de-throned,
and keeps the rags of lordship once he owned:
Man, Sub-creator, the refracted Light
through whom is splintered from a single White
to many hues, and endlessly combined
in living shapes that move from mind to mind.
Though all the crannies of the world we filled
with Elves and Goblins, though we dared to build
Gods and their houses out of dark and light,
and sowed the seed of dragons—'twas our right
(used or misused). That right has not decayed:
we make still by the law in which we're made."
(OFS, p. 74)

For all its brevity, more is contained in this poem than
in the earlier prose passage; its ramifications spread further.
The third line—" 'Dis-graced he may be, yet is not dethroned' "—is a near repetition of a line from the *Beowulf*
essay, the line referring to "man fallen and not yet saved,
disgraced but not dethroned." The conscious repetition of the
two key words and the addition of the hyphens to clarify the
reference suggest a link between the two essays. And its new
context in the poem gives the phrase even greater force than
it carried in the *Beowulf* essay. There it was used to characterize pagan yet noble man, doomed to find his only glory
in the losing battle against the monsters. Here it refers to
sub-creative man, making rather than fighting, fallen—yes—
but not dethroned, still the child of God and capable, like his
Creator, of creating.

In the poem as opposed to the prose passage, Tolkien
emphasizes man's *right* to sub-create; not just to make, but
to make by the law " 'in which we're made.' " The preposition here is worth noting: we are not made *by* a law, but *in*
that law. We are part of it, not just products of it. That law
is the word, the Logos, the expression of Barfield's whole
vision, fragmented as we have fallen, and as our perception
has fragmented. Making by that law in which we're made—
the word—we have " 'dared to build/Gods and their houses

out of dark and light,' " a polarity which adumbrates the theme of The Silmarillion.

Finally, and perhaps most important, there is the image of the Light splintered from the original White to "many hues" as it is refracted through the sub-creative mind of man. This last change from the prose passage is the most crucial, for it shifts the medium of creation. Man is still the sub-creator, but his material now is light rather than word. The process of sub-creation is the splintering or refracting and re-combining of light to create those " 'living shapes that move from mind to mind,' " whereas in the prose passage it was the combining of words, the incantatory use of adjectival phrases in a mythical grammar.

The shift from words to light appears to be a shift from the literal to the metaphoric. Moreover, the metaphor seems at first to be an unlikely one. But if we look at it closely, we will see that Tolkien is using words with that awareness of their earliest meaning which is his characteristic. In this case he is invoking precisely that mythic literality which Barfield's concept of ancient semantic unity postulates, and the fact that he does so makes his ready acceptance of Barfield's theory clear.

Both words and light are agents of perception, enabling us to see phenomena. The word for a thing—the name—governs how it is perceived. Something instinctive in the use of language reaches for metaphors of light to convey mental as well as physical perception. We clarify an argument. We say we see when we mean we understand. A change in wording can put things in a different light. Three uses of this kind of metaphor occur in the previous paragraph alone. This is nothing new; any study of language turns up such dead metaphor all the time. The point is that for Tolkien it is neither dead nor a metaphor—it is a living reality. For him the Word is Light, enlightenment.

In both passages of his essay Tolkien is addressing himself to the writing of fantasy. He has already equated fantasy with Coleridge's Imagination, and with "freedom from observed fact." For the perceiving mind with its faculty of imagination, there is much more than mere facts to be observed in this or any other world. Appearances must be interpreted;

and certainly there is more than one way of seeing things. The word *fantasy*, which for Tolkien is so important, is etymologically linked to the word *phenomena*, and both have to do with appearances and perception. *Phenomena* is the word for the appearances of the Primary World, appearances revealed by light, fixed as concepts by words. *Fantasy* involves the making of a Secondary World, the appearances of which are built up in words.

Both terms—*phenomena* and *fantasy*—derive from Greek. *Phenomena* comes from *phainesthai*, "to appear." *Fantasy* comes from *phantazein*, "to make visible." The difference between them lies in the activity or passivity of the thing appearing: *phenomena/phainesthai* appears, whereas *fantasy/phantazein* causes to appear. Both come from the earlier Greek word *phainein*, "to show," which, as the earlier and less distinct concept, must pre-date the active/passive distinction, separating by word things which appear from that which makes things appear. Much the same concept is contained in all three words. Moreover, the separation indicated by the two later words illustrates that very fragmentation of a prior unified concept which Barfield postulates. The further back in time, the closer to whole the concept appears. And the earliest concept leads directly to light, for all three words—*phainesthai, phantazein,* and *phainein*—can be traced back to Indo-European *bhā-*[1], "to shine." It would seem, then, that there must have been a time during man's development of language when *phenomena* and *fantasy*—"appearances perceived" and "appearances shaped by imagination"—must have been more closely linked, less immediately distinguishable from one another than they are today. Deriving, as they do, from *bhā-*[1], both words carry some concept of bearing or reflecting light. It can hardly be coincidence that the entry directly after *bhā-*[1] in the dictionary is Indo-European *bhā-*[2], a root with the same spelling and the same sound, meaning "to speak," from which comes Greek *phōnē*, "sound, voice," developing into *phōnein*, "to sound, speak," and then into *phōnēma*, "an utterance." Thus, phonologically at least, light and word can be linked, traced back to the same sound. We are at liberty to speculate that there may have been at one time a semantic link as well, implying a perceptual connection. This much is clear: phenomena and fantasy, related kinds of appearance, can be revealed by light or by word, and perhaps in an earlier, more unified sense by light as word, at once the instrument and expression of man's perception of his world.

Both light and word, then, as Tolkien sees them, can be instruments of sub-creation. Light, however, pushes the concept further than does word. The White Light of the poem recalls the White Light of God which Tolkien envisioned as holding the mote. But in the poem man is not the mote; he is instead the prism through which the White Light passes and is splintered into the hues of the color spectrum. The parallel to Barfield's theory of the splintering of meaning is clear; indeed, if we can accept the light/word correspondence suggested by phenomena/fantasy and $bh\bar{a}$-[1] and $bh\bar{a}$-[2], we can see Tolkien and Barfield as more than parallel, as addressing the same process through related manifestations. Man, splintering light to many hues, splintering original perception into many concepts and words, is using fantasy to particularize and make manifest fragments of original truth.

For Tolkien, profoundly Christian and devoutly Catholic, all three elements—man, light, and truth—have their origin in God. In acting as a prism and thus refracting light and word, "Man, Sub-creator" is fulfilling God's purpose by making a fantasy world which will of necessity reflect the phenomena of our world. Sub-creation is not idle or random imitation of God; it is part of His intent.

That this was Tolkien's view of sub-creation is clear from his words in the last paragraph of the fairy-story essay. When he has dealt with *evangelium* and Joy, and explored the relationship between fairy-story and the Christian story, between Creation and Sub-creation, he brings all together in his concluding statement:

> The Christian has still to work, with mind as well as body, to suffer, hope, and die; but he may now perceive that all his bents and faculties have a purpose, which

> can be redeemed. So great is the bounty with which he
> has been treated that he may now, perhaps, fairly dare
> to guess that in Fantasy he may actually assist in the
> effoliation and multiple enrichment of creation. All
> tales may come true; and yet, at the last, redeemed,
> they may be as like and unlike the forms we give them
> as Man, finally redeemed, will be like and unlike the
> fallen that we know. (OFS, pp. 89-90)

This line of thought extends Tolkien's theory to its ultimate. Such extension and the reasoning behind it are very
much in the same spirit as Barfield's continuing exploration
of the fragmentation of meaning, and the function and purpose of that fragmentation as he develops them in his later
books and lectures. Beyond the already-discussed response
which Tolkien had to *Poetic Diction*, there is no evidence
that Tolkien was acquainted with Barfield's other books,
which expand and deepen his theory of the relationship of
language and perception. But no further reading of Barfield
would really have been necessary for Tolkien, because Barfield has said of his own work that however many books and
articles he has written, he is "really saying the same thing
over and over again."[6] It seems clear that the two men shared
a community of mind and a community of interests. Beyond
that, each seems to have reached independently much the
same perspective on the development of man and language.

Both Tolkien and Barfield saw the Word as the instrument of Creation, and words as instruments and indices of
man's separation from God and from the universe. And both
felt that the task of the poet was to bridge that separation.
For each of them, words are to be the poetic instruments of
man's ultimate and conscious re-union with God. Barfield
makes it clear that man feels and expresses his separation in
and by words, and that through the creative power of the
word man can return. The poet, through his use of metaphor,
is a maker of meaning and a re-creator of perception. He re-
invests the world with meaning and rebuilds man's relation-

---

[6]Owen Barfield, *The Rediscovery of Meaning and Other Essays* (Middletown, Conn.: Wesleyan University Press, 1977), p. 3.

ship with it. Surely this is splintered light "endlessly combined," that mythical grammar by which Tolkien's sub-creator may assist in the "effoliation and multiple enrichment of creation."

To turn from Tolkien's essay to The Silmarillion is to go from theory to practice. The work is a vast, fantasy mythology with the familiar mythological themes—gods and men, creation, transgression, love, war, heroism, and doom. But more than anything else, and more than most mythologies, it is a story about light. Images of light in all stages—brilliant, dim, whole, refracted—pervade the songs and stories of Tolkien's fictive world, a world peopled by sub-creators whose interactions with the light shape Middle-earth and their own destinies. Tolkien's use of light in The Silmarillion derives from his Christian belief and takes its method from Barfield's theory. His approach is to first restore to words their primal unity of concept and then to set up progressive fragmentation as they express a continuing relationship to the world and a continuing reflection of the light. His technique is to confer literality on what now would be called metaphor and then to illustrate the process by which the literal becomes metaphoric.

To understand how this works we must know something about the elements of Tolkien's fantasy world. As might be expected, its structure recalls the general structure of the major Western mythologies, both pagan and Christian. There is above all a First Cause, Eru, with the epithet Ilúvatar. In Tolkien's elven language the element *er* means "one, alone,"[7] and the name Eru is translated as "The One." The likeness of Tolkien's *er* to Indo-European *er-*[1], "to set in motion," and its similarity to the related Germanic *ar-*, "to be, exist," are hard to ignore. Possible relationships between fanciful languages and known ones should be approached with caution, for there can be no real, generic connection. Nevertheless, given Tolkien's knowledge of the roots of language, we may

---

[7]J.R.R. Tolkien, *The Silmarillion,* ed. Christopher Tolkien (Boston: Houghton Mifflin, 1977), p. 358. Hereafter page references will be cited parenthetically in the text, with this abbreviation: *TS.*

at least take note of the obvious similarity, both in sound and meaning, between elven *er* and the Indo-European and Germanic roots. Eru, "The One," is the Prime Mover from whom all existence flows.

The epithet Ilúvatar relates to how he is perceived, for it is the name given him by his created beings, the elves, and in their language means "Allfather" or "Father of All." Just below Eru in the hierarchy are the Ainur, "the Holy Ones," described as products of his thought. Tolkien's concept of them as "products" of "The One" suggests a sort of Pythagorean division of unity into multiplicity. They are powers or principalities emanating directly from the godhead, and seem to be aspects of his nature. Creation comes about when Eru propounds a musical theme to the Ainur, inviting them to embellish it and make music. In this music the world is born.

A variety of peoples inhabit this world, but two races predominate—elves and men. Both races embody aspects of humankind, and in their continually changing relationship to light Tolkien explores man's relationship to God. A problem of nomenclature arises here, in just how to refer to Tolkien's peoples. He clearly intended elves and men to be two distinct species, yet it is also plain that he intended them to represent different aspects of the human race. Tolkien's own comments about both races make this obvious. He wrote of elves, "Of course in reality . . . my 'elves' are only a representation or an apprehension of a part of human nature . . ." (*TLOT*, p. 149), and again, ". . . I should say that they represent really Men with greatly enhanced aesthetic and creative faculties, greater beauty and longer life . . ." (*TLOT*, p. 176). Of both elves and men he wrote:

> Of course, in fact exterior to my story, Elves and Men are just different aspects of the Humane, and represent the problem of death as seen by a finite but willing and self-conscious person. In this mythological world the Elves and Men are in their incarnate forms kindred, but in the relation of their 'spirits' to the world in time represent different 'experiments', each of which has its own natural trend and weakness. (*TLOT*, p. 236)

The problem intrudes when elves and men must be referred to together, when it becomes necessary to find a term which will encompass both and yet leave it clear that they are separate. Something of the same complication arises with respect to men and hobbits. Tolkien says of these two: "The Hobbits are, of course, really meant to be a branch of the specifically *human* race (not Elves or Dwarves) . . ." (*TLOT*, p. 158). Here he classes hobbits with men as human and excludes elves. Presented thus with three distinct groups, all of which are described as human at one time or another, two of which are compared with men but not with each other, the reader can be excused for experiencing some confusion. The niceties of distinction among elves, men, and hobbits, clear enough in reference to any one of the three, begin to blur when it becomes necessary to generalize about them in relation to their creator, or in comparison with real human beings. "Humanity" will not do; it is too broad a term. The difficulty may be resolved by classing elves and men (separately and together) as humankind, and men and hobbits (separately and together) as mankind.

The differences between the two races are central to Tolkien's purpose, for these differences directly affect the relationship of each to Eru and to the world around them. The most striking difference is that men die and leave the world, whereas elves do not. Tolkien commented a number of times (most often in his letters) that the theme of his work was death and immortality. One citation, representative of many, will illustrate the point:

> The real theme for me is about something much more permanent and difficult [than war]: Death and Immortality: the mystery of the love of the world in the hearts of a race 'doomed' to leave and seemingly lose it; the anguish in the hearts of a race 'doomed' not to leave it, until its whole evil-aroused story is complete. (*TLOT*, p. 246)

Within the mythology, death is called Ilúvatar's gift to men, a gift whose value is distorted and made to seem evil by the dark powers. Beyond this "gift," men have another power granted them: the power to act beyond the creational design of the Music.

This capability unmistakably introduces free will into the design and parallels the light/dark paradox with a fate/free-will polarity which increases the tension of the world. Some confusion may arise here, however, as to just how specific Tolkien intended to be in his allocation of fate, contained in the Music, and the power to change fate which he gives to men. No such power is given to elves, and the Music is plainly described as being "as fate" to all things but men, and thus presumably to elves. Yet at one or two points in *The Silmarillion* Tolkien describes situations in which elves have a choice between good and evil. A possible distinction may be that Eru has given to men the power to *act* beyond the Music (that is, to change external events) and to elves the freedom to make an inner choice, to alter some attitude toward themselves, or other creatures, or God. While elves may not alter events, they may have power over their own natures.

In a letter to a reviewer of *The Lord of the Rings,* Tolkien wrote that both races were "rational creatures of free will in regard to God" (*TLOT*, p. 236). The key may lie in the phrase "in regard to God," which suggests that in Tolkien's world God is beyond and above fate. This implies a concept in which the mind of God exceeds any design perceivable by any of His creatures. A striking statement by a character in *Unfinished Tales* supports this view. He is one of the Ainur, one of the products of Eru's thought, and thus an aspect of him. It can be assumed, then, that he speaks for him, and for Tolkien as well:

> 'But behold!' said he, 'in the armour of Fate (as the Children of Earth name it) there is ever a rift, and in the walls of Doom a breach, until the full-making, which ye call the End. So it shall be while I endure, a secret voice that gainsayeth, and a light where darkness was decreed. Therefore, though in the days of this darkness I seem to oppose the will of my brethren, the Lords of the West, that is my part among them, to which I was appointed ere the making of the World.'[8]

---

[8]J.R.R. Tolkien, *Unfinished Tales of Númenor and Middle-earth,* ed. Christopher Tolkien (Boston: Houghton Mifflin, 1980), p. 29.

This seems to make it clear that in Tolkien's cosmology, which encompasses both fate and free will, the mind of the Prime Mover goes beyond the Creation, and leaves room for what to earthbound perceivers may appear as exceptions to the rule. Within the narrative Tolkien is content to illustrate this concept. Elsewhere, he states it explicitly:

> Free Will is derivative, and is only operative within provided circumstances; but in order that it may exist, it is necessary that the Author should guarantee it, whatever betides: sc. when it is 'against His will', as we say, at any rate as it appears on a finite view. (*TLOT*, p. 195)

Within the mythology, Eru's gift of free will to men is only "operative within provided circumstances," that is, within the Music. Elsewhere, Tolkien writes of "the Finger of God, as the one wholly free Will and Agent" (*TLOT*, p. 204).

As far as action goes, Eru is a remote and disengaged God figure. He has little or no direct interaction in his world, leaving it to those of the Ainur called the Valar, the Powers of the World, who choose to concern themselves specifically with the earth and its inhabitants. Tolkien describes them as "angelic powers, whose function is to exercise delegated authority in their spheres," and as "divine," that is, existing before the creation of the world. Within the narrative they function as limited god-figures. Tolkien explains: "On the side of mere narrative device, this is, of course, meant to provide beings of the same order of beauty, power, and majesty as the 'gods' of higher mythology, which can yet be accepted—well, shall we say baldly, by a mind that believes in the Blessed Trinity" (*TLOT*, p. 146).

The concept of the Valar is particularly important to Tolkien's cosmology. While their position in the hierarchy certainly suggests angelic beings, their role in the scheme of things is, from a strictly Christian point of view, eccentric. Tolkien's treatment of them, the powers for good and evil which he gives them, takes them a good way beyond the conventional view of angels. They are makers, or sub-creators, who work with and within the fabric of the world to shape it. In that capacity they seem more directly comparable to the God of Genesis (chapter one), the Elohim, than is Eru. It is worth noting, but not emphasizing here, that *Elohim*, which the King James Bible renders *God*, is technically a plural intensive of the Hebrew *El*, "God," and thus could suggest more than one, or God in all His aspects. But Tolkien never allows the comparison to be specific or explicit. His Valar, he says, "take the imaginative but not the theological place of 'gods' " (*TLOT*, p. 284). Manwë, the chief of the Valar, is lord of the earth, and Eru's deputy. His epithet is Súlimo, "The Breather," and he is master of the airs and winds, lord of the airs of Arda, the world. Both in function and in epithet—that is, as he is perceived—Manwë thus encompasses all the ancient meanings of *spiritus* and *pneuma* cited by Barfield: "breath," "wind," and "spirit." And this also ties him to Genesis, in which the spirit of God moves upon the waters. Hebrew *ruach*, rendered *spirit* in the King James, also means "breath." Manwë thus has a function not unlike that of God as He is conventionally viewed, although Tolkien makes it clear that he is not God but a secondary figure.

The word Tolkien uses to describe the labors of the Valar in making the world is "demiurgic." The adjective recalls Plato's use of the same word to describe the deity who fashions the material world, and the Gnostic designation of a "demiurge" as the creator of the material world. Certainly the Valar create Tolkien's material world, which puts them far closer to the role of God than to that of the angels. But Tolkien's concept of God is figured in Eru, and the difference between Eru and the Valar is crucial to an understanding of Tolkien's view of God. There is only one Creator—Eru, the One. The Ainur, the Valar, are sub-creators. They take part in the physical making of the world, but could not have done so had not Eru first given them the theme. Tolkien states clearly that "the whole matter from beginning to end is mainly concerned with the relation of Creation to making and sub-creation" (*TLOT*, p. 188), and says of Creation: "The act of Will of Eru the One that gives Reality to conceptions, is distinguished from making, which is permissive" (*TLOT*, p. 190).

Sub-creation, then, is demiurgic. And here again etymology may clarify Tolkien's purpose. The word *demiurge* can be traced to two Indo-European roots: *dā-*, "to divide," and *werg-* [1], "to do." Assuming an early unitary meaning, we can speculate that *demiurge* may have encompassed several concepts—"to divide in doing," "to do *by* dividing," and "to do by *being* divided." The word can thus be read as describing both the Valar and their labor. As products of Eru's thought, they themselves are divisions, aspects, splinters of Eru, parts of his wholeness. And in making the world (in an echo of the God of Genesis dividing the waters from the dry land), they are dividing it into its components—air, water, earth—and thus separating wholeness into parts. But they are also dividing the world *from* Eru, and assisting in a process of separation whereby Eru and the world can contemplate each other. The similarity between this dramatic enactment and Barfield's philological theory is clear.

The Valar are also made to suggest the gods of pagan mythologies, since they have separate functions and each has a particular role in, or association with, an element of the earth—air, water, minerals, growing things. Some are associated with theoretical concepts, such as judgment or fate. Under them are lesser Valar called Maiar, who seem to be more local and suggest inhabiting spirits.

The keynote in Tolkien's vision of the world is his concept of creation. Music is the initiating force and the beginning in which all is contained. Eru propounds a musical theme to the Ainur and invites them to elaborate it and make from it a Great Music. It is the first action, and brings with it the first conflict, for in the making of the Music the first rebellion occurs. Melkor, the greatest of the Ainur and the closest to Eru, is not content to serve Eru's theme, and counters with a theme of his own. The result is a kind of war in heaven—two Musics in contention with one another, one melodious and harmonic, the other clamorous and discordant.

The reference is obvious, but the noteworthy aspect is the blending of two distinct ideas to make a coherent and dramatic whole. The first is the rebellion of Lucifer, which is embedded in Christian thought through the Bible and even more through Milton's *Paradise Lost*. The second is the concept of heavenly harmony and of music as the ordering force in the universe. A viable concept throughout the Middle Ages, it persisted as a metaphor well into the eighteenth century, informing, for example, Dryden's "St. Cecilia's Day Ode." Tolkien has taken these two ideas—war in heaven and cosmic harmony—and woven them together, making each dependent on the other and, what is more important, making them *reality*. Rebellion is disharmony, but in this fantasy world the disharmony is literal and actual.

A clear difference is apparent here between Tolkien's myth and the Christian mythology which underlies it. The difference is deliberate, and is part of Tolkien's effort to remove any overt Christianity from his cosmology, lest it become too explicit and too readily recognizable. The Christian elements are there, but Tolkien has modified or re-worked them so that they may recall Christianity, but still pertain specifically to his sub-created *mythos*. He wrote of this:

> I suppose a difference between this Myth and what may be perhaps called Christian mythology is this. In the latter the Fall of Man is subsequent to and a consequence (though not a necessary consequence) of the 'Fall of the Angels': a rebellion of created free-will at a higher level than Man; but it is not clearly held (and in many versions is not held at all) that this affected the 'World' in its nature: evil was brought in from outside, by Satan. In this Myth the rebellion of created free-will precedes creation of the world (Eä); and Eä has in it, subcreatively introduced, evil, rebellions, discordant elements of its own nature already when the *Let it Be* was spoken. The Fall or corruption, therefore, of all things in it and all inhabitants of it, was a possibility if not inevitable. (*TLOT*, pp. 286-287)

Melkor's disharmony becomes an active part of the Music, and so the rebellion affects the shape of the world that is to be. For the Music is not the physical act of creation; rather, it is pattern, the world *in potentia*. The vision evoked by the Music is shown to the Ainur, including Melkor. Their task is to go down into the world and make real the pattern in response to Eru's commanding Word: " '*Eä*! Let these things Be!' " (*TS*, p. 20).

It seems clear that in this invention of the music Tolkien is consciously synthesizing and building on the two biblical accounts of creation, one in Genesis and the other in the Gospel according to Saint John. Genesis begins with God's call for light; Saint John declares that in the beginning was the Word. As we have seen, *word, logos,* meant at one time far more than it does today. It carried the force of harmony, order, principle of organization; it meant something very close to music. For Tolkien, as for medieval man, light and music are conjoined elements manifest in the music of the spheres, the singing of the stars. The word *Eä,* which in Elvish means "it is" or "let it be," becomes the imperative of the Great Music, the vision which is both light and *logos.*

The importance and power of the word for Tolkien cannot be too strongly emphasized. Philological essays such as "*Sigelwara Land*" and "Chaucer as a Philologist" are evidence of the painstaking care he took with the words of a text, sifting through orthography and sound change, re-constructing where possible, in order to come as close as the modern mind can come to the original meaning and original use. In his valedictory address to the University of Oxford on the occasion of his retirement as Merton Professor of English Language and Literature, he characterized his work as scholar and teacher: "I would always rather try to wring the juice out of a single sentence, or explore the implications of one word than try to sum up a period in a lecture, or pot a poet in a paragraph."[9] The Silmarillion is testimony to his desire to "explore the implications of one word," for the whole vast sweep of his mythology is in truth just that—the exploration of the implications and ramifications of the one word *Eä.*

The Valar must realize the implications of *Eä,* for as Eru

---

[9]J.R.R. Tolkien, "Valedictory Address to the University of Oxford, 5 June 1959," in *J.R.R. Tolkien: Scholar and Storyteller—Essays in Memoriam,* ed. Mary Salu and Robert Farrell (Ithaca: Cornell University Press, 1979), p. 17.

speaks it, the world is only potential. Entering into the world, the Valar find that the real work is still to be done:

> ... for it was as if naught was yet made which they had seen in vision, and all was but on point to begin and yet unshaped, and it was dark. For the Great Music had been but the growth and flowering of thought in the Timeless Halls, and the Vision only a foreshowing; but now they had entered in at the beginning of Time, and the Valar perceived that the World had been but foreshadowed and foresung, and they must achieve it. (TS, p. 20)

The task of the Valar is to shape and light the world, but the whole concept is Eru's. In fulfilling Eru's purpose they are already once removed from his wholeness, for they bring to the world not light but lights, a variety of lights of different kinds and lessening intensities. Each light is dimmer than the last, splintered by Tolkien's sub-creators.

This extended image of light diminished from its primal brilliance, yet still faintly illuminating the world, is paralleled by Tolkien's presentation of the peoples of that world and their language. More and more, as the story progresses, we are shown through character, deed, and word that elves and men are, in their different ways, drawn to the light and yet separated from it. The work is permeated by an air of deepening sorrow, of loss and estrangement, and ever-widening distance from the light and all that it means. Tolkien has invented a world and its people through which to explore the meaning and consequences of the Fall—that long separation of mankind from the light of God.

By making light a tangible reality and putting it in the hands of a succession of sub-creators, Tolkien is inviting his reader to experience the newly created world of The Silmarillion as Barfield suggests early man experienced his world. What we might be tempted to separate into levels of meaning—literal, metaphoric, symbolic—is presented as a vital whole, a re-creation of that original participation of man with his world which Barfield postulates. This is a mythic mode of thought, and in a world where such a mode is no longer dominant, we must call it fantasy. The realistic novel, deriving from and describing a world in which mythic thinking is largely out of fashion, is unable to present such material believably. The natural vehicle is fantasy; the best and most persuasive method is sub-creation.

Such sub-creation, however, should not be attempted lightly, for if it fails to persuade, to induce in the reader the enchanted state of secondary belief, the results will be at best shallowly commercial, and at worst laughable. Good sub-creation must be built on that "inner consistency of reality" which Tolkien describes in the fairy-story essay. "Anyone," he says, "inheriting the fantastic device of human language can say *the green sun.* Many can then imagine or picture it. But that is not enough. . . . To make a Secondary World inside which the green sun will be credible, commanding Secondary Belief, will probably require labour and thought, and will certainly demand a special skill, a kind of elvish craft" (OFS, p. 70).

At the risk of belaboring a point, let me call attention to Tolkien's use of the word *fantastic* to describe human language. He is talking about the writing of fantasy, but he takes it as a given that human language is a "device" peculiarly designed for the creation of fantasy. Used literally, of course, the word *fantastic* will mean "revealing or throwing light on appearances," and we have seen that for Tolkien this is a primary function of language. The use of so powerful a tool must be backed up by conscious effort, and must be informed by skill beyond the ordinary, what he calls an "elvish craft."

Tolkien is, of course, talking about himself, for he was well aware of his own extraordinary skill. His "green sun" in The Silmarillion is the light. His "elvish craft" is his ability to create with language. And in his case "language" as a term must be extended beyond the English language in which his work is written, though he uses English consciously, and it is always important. But "language" means also his invented languages—the primary Elvish and its derivatives—spoken by the peoples of his fantastic world. Tolkien has said that he created his world as the background and justification for those invented languages which had been his hobby since childhood. Language came first, and his development of it forced him to realize that there can be no language without a people who speak it, no people without a culture which expresses them, no culture without a myth which informs and shapes it. His own "inner consistency of reality," then, is one in which myth, language, and culture reflect one another. His Secondary World is one in which his particular green sun—light as concrete reality embodying the felt presence of the spiritual—is not only credible but inevitable.

The basis of his work is the language. It permeates the story, builds the world, colors events, shapes character, and supports and embodies the theme. To fully explore this, however, we must go back before language and begin with the time in Tolkien's world when the Valar are making concrete the pattern of the Music. And here "language" and "speech" must be qualified. Eru "speaks" to the Ainur, and Tolkien frequently shows the Ainur in "speech" with one another. But it seems clear that this is meant to be taken as pre-verbal, as some kind of supersensible communication among spiritual beings. The nearest Tolkien comes to suggesting language among the Ainur is in his description of their Music: "Then the voices of the Ainur, like unto harps and lutes, and pipes and trumpets, and viols and organs, and like unto countless choirs singing with words, began to fashion the theme of Ilúvatar to a great music" (TS, p. 15). The phrase "singing with words" might imply speech but for the modifying phrase "like unto," which precedes all the instruments listed. Speech is pre-figured; in Tolkien's words it is "foreshadowed and foresung," as is the rest of creation, but at this point in the narrative it is not an actuality. *Speech* as the word is commonly used—the exercise of vocal muscles to produce meaningful human sound—begins well after the creation of the world, and is introduced into Middle-earth by the elves. Predictably, it comes out of light.

The shape of the earth, twisted from its original pattern by Melkor's rebellion against Eru, is altered again in the actual making. The quarrelsome Melkor contends again with the other Valar for dominion in the shaping of the earth. At every turn he mars the work, destroying what the others create, tearing down what they build up, undoing or changing every effort. After a time he is defeated, but his war has marked the world.

When order is restored, Yavanna, goddess of growing things, plants the earth with seeds. It is at this point in creation that light as a necessity is introduced. Then, says the narrator, "there was need of light" (*TS*, p. 35). In Middle-earth, as in our own world, there can be no growth without light.

> Aulë at the prayer of Yavanna wrought two mighty lamps for the lighting of the Middle-earth which he had built amid the encircling seas. Then Varda [Queen of the Valar] filled the lamps and Manwë hallowed them, and the Valar set them upon high pillars, more lofty far than are any mountains of the later days. One lamp they raised near to the north of Middle-earth, and it was named Illuin; and the other was raised in the south, and it was named Ormal; and the light of the Lamps of the Valar flowed out over the Earth, so that all was lit as it were in a changeless day. (*TS*, p. 35)

This first of the lights seems to be something not far removed from the primal light of God. It is brilliant and constant; there is no night, no dark. Light (and therefore truth) is ever-present and all-illuminating. But this state of things cannot last, because strife is in the Music and strife shapes the events of the world. Coming forth suddenly, Melkor throws down the pillars and breaks the Lamps. In the tumult of their overthrow the shapes of land and sea are changed again. Flame from the Lamps spills out and scorches the land, and in the lovely but imperfect and discordant world of Middle-earth the uncontained light and heat are too intense— they destroy what they touch. Thus the first light is put out and cannot be renewed.

After a time new light is brought into being, but the quality is changed and the brilliance diminished. Yavanna calls forth light, but since her province is nature and growing things, not the air and fire which are the provinces of Manwë and Varda, this light is different in kind from the primal, fiery element of the Lamps. Through Yavanna's singing the two

Trees Laurelin and Telperion come into being. Again the relationship of light and music is evoked, but in diminished terms. The music is now a single voice, not a cosmic choir, and the light itself is dimmer, no longer all-illuminating.

The differences between the Lamps and the Trees are striking, and conform to the pattern of diminution which underlies the mythology. Where the Lamps lighted all of Middle-earth, the Trees shine only in Valinor, home of the Valar. Moreover, theirs is a softer light, a gold and silver glow, rather than an intense, unshielded flame. Rooted in the natural world, the Trees give light in waxing and waning cycles of flower and fruit. Each shines in turn for seven hours, and the waning hour of each is the awakening hour of the other, so that periodically the gold and silver lights overlap and glow in concert. The concept is an extraordinarily beautiful one, but the beauty is functional, serving the theme. These cycles of light mark the beginning of days, an alternation of light which suggests measured time. There is still no night, no absolute dark, but there is a hesitation and pulsation, as if the light now must be tempered, filtered through the life of the world, and brought softly into being. Nevertheless, this is the light of the world. Tolkien wrote of it: "The light of Valinor (derived from light before any fall) is the light of art undivorced from reason, that sees things both scientifically (or philosophically) and imaginatively (or subcreatively) and 'says that they are good'—as beautiful" (*TLOT*, p. 148).

While there is still light in Valinor, Middle-earth now is dark, benighted save for the stars, dim, inaccessible points of light beyond reach. Even before the earth is peopled the light is withdrawn. With this development we can clearly see how Tolkien uses fantasy to re-invest metaphor with literality. Those who seek the light can find it, but they must be shown the way. In Middle-earth, as in our own world, enlightenment is to be desired, but in Middle-earth it is a physical reality, not just a metaphor for an inner state of being, and to find it one must physically exchange darkness for light. Thus a decision to exchange one state of being for another entails action, not just a change of heart or mind.

This diminution of light cannot yet be called a splintering, although it prefigures splintering in the lessening and the subtle introduction of color, which come with the shift from the Lamps to the Trees. The next interaction of sub-creator and light, however, is a true splintering, and it presages the beginning of speech in Tolkien's world. The two Trees not only radiate light, they exude it as a kind of dew, which falls from each tree and is caught in vats. From the gathered dew of the silver Tree, Telperion, Varda fashions new and brighter stars so that the elves, when they awaken in Middle-earth, may have some fragments of the light. This is clearly to be seen as a sub-creative splintering of light, for Varda is breaking wholeness into parts and using those parts to reveal a world, however dimly.

Her purpose is to prepare for the awakening of the first true inhabitants of Middle-earth, the first people. While they are to be seen as humankind, albeit supra-human in their beauty and power, Tolkien's treatment of their coming is notably unlike that of most mythologies in that there is no "first elf," no primordial ancestor from whom the race springs. The elves arise as a group—as a group they are created, as a group they awaken, and as a group they respond to the light of Varda's stars.

The next step is speech, and here Tolkien vividly and dramatically realizes Barfield's theory of language. For it is with and through speech and word that the elves come to recognize themselves, and to create for themselves that world of which they are a part yet separate. From the primal first spoken word to the many languages of Middle-earth we can trace precisely that development of perception and growing awareness of self and phenomena as separate entities which Barfield postulates.

The elves and their language now become Tolkien's chief instruments of sub-creation. Through their burgeoning and progressively fragmenting awareness of themselves and their world, Middle-earth comes to life before our eyes. From ancient unity to the fragmentation and splintering of light, of perception, of society and of self, Tolkien's sub-created world mirrors our own, and through its people, their wars and turmoils, their triumphs and disasters, we come gradually to recognize ourselves, to see and hear ourselves as Tolkien hears and sees us. In showing us his world Tolkien has enabled us to recover our own, to know ourselves as we were and are, so that we may have some glimpse, however dim, of what we may yet be.

IV
A DISEASE OF MYTHOLOGY

*To ask what is the origin of stories . . . is to ask
what is the origin of language and of the mind.*

TOLKIEN, "ON FAIRY-STORIES"

We come now to the heart of the matter for both Barfield
and Tolkien, and that is language. However idly Tolkien may
have begun the invention of languages as a hobby, as his
concept of mythology grew he came to regard it as no mere
exercise but as the index of a world, the agent and reflection
of its cultural development, and the repository of its myth
and history. The languages of Middle-earth, in their development, are so striking an illustration of Barfield's thesis that
one might almost think Tolkien had kept *Poetic Diction* at
his elbow as he worked. Both "On Fairy-stories" and The
Silmarillion contain what would seem to be clear references
to specific points of Barfield's argument.

In the fourth chapter of *Poetic Diction,* "Meaning and
Myth," Barfield argues for his concept of ancient semantic
unity against the then-current view of the German philologist Max Müller. Müller held that man's use of language involved extracting meaning from already-existing concepts and
applying it to observed phenomena in a conscious, intellectual process of metaphorization and myth-formation. Müller
went so far as to call mythology "a disease of language," a
phrase which aroused the ire, or at least the disagreement, of
both Barfield and Tolkien. To illustrate the conscious process
at work in the making of metaphor, the way in which myth
could be seen as "a disease of language," Müller gave as an
example what he called the "root" meaning "to shine." Such
a "root," he theorized, was first applied to concrete phenom-

ena such as fire and the sun, and then quite consciously extended into metaphor to express the effect of spring, morning light, and the like.

Müller's view is now largely discredited by the work of Cassirer, Lévy-Bruhl, and others, and it may seem contrived to resurrect an outdated argument in order to show it up. But familiarity with Müller's theory is important to an understanding of the thought processes of both Barfield and Tolkien, for they both used him as a kind of negative point of departure, as the chief spokesman of a view against which they would argue their own, directly contrary point of view. Barfield was one of the first serious students of the history of words to take issue with Müller, and Tolkien places himself firmly on Barfield's side. Barfield argues that "to shine," far from being a root which sprouted a multitude of meanings, must have had an original meaning which encompassed all the phenomena, both concrete and metaphoric, which Müller cited. It was, Barfield argues, "not an empty root meaning 'to shine', but the same definite spiritual reality which was beheld on the one hand in what has since become pure human thinking; and on the other hand, in what has since become physical light" (*PD*, p. 88).

Tolkien makes substantially the same argument in "On Fairy-stories." Writing some ten years after the publication of *Poetic Diction*, he also takes on Max Müller. Indeed, he makes a special point to quote Müller's description of mythology as a disease of language so that he may propose the reverse: mythology is not a disease of language; languages are a disease of mythology (OFS, p. 48). In making this pronouncement, Tolkien may well have been thinking of his own invented languages as well as the European ones to which he refers in the essay. The word *disease*, suggesting as it does an abnormal or pathological state, is an uncomfortable term for language, but Tolkien means it literally. Dis-ease, discomfort, whether painful or pleasurable, leads to consciousness, and consciousness leads to language. Language arises out of mythology, not the other way round. For Tolkien, as for Barfield, language is not a set of abstract concepts applied at will to phenomena, like a coat of paint; rather, it is the expression of perception of living reality in all its manifestations. Language is the outgrowth of and the agent for mythic perception. Language and myth are interrelated manifestations of burgeoning consciousness, of awareness of a world.

The path from "Meaning and Myth" through "On Fairy-stories" to The Silmarillion is a short, straight road. In "On Fairy-stories" Tolkien follows Barfield in arguing against Max Müller. In The Silmarillion he uses "to shine," the specific example over which Barfield disagreed with Müller, as the formative mythological and philological concept for the fiction. The Silmarillion is all about light, light treated in just the manner which Barfield postulates: something which begins as "a definite spiritual reality," becomes divided into "pure human thinking" and "physical light," and ultimately splinters, both as percept and as word, into myriad fragments, all of which serve to characterize Tolkien's world and those who inhabit it.

That polarity of light and dark which defines the physical and spiritual realities of Tolkien's world is both mirrored in and codified by the developing languages of Middle-earth. Inspired by light and imbued with the consciousness of its meaning, elven language, in its fragmentation from whole perception into many views and tongues, illustrates precisely the principle of splintered light which Tolkien makes the guiding image of his "Mythopoeia" poem. Moreover, the splintering process, for all that it breaks up and diffuses the whole, the White Light, gives rise to the beauty of all the colors, and makes possible light of many hues. Since Tolkien so firmly links light and language, this must then be equally true of language. Splintering of perception leads to narrowed but also more precise expression, greater variety in the play of words, and an infinite variety of combinations in that "mythical grammar" which is the instrument of sub-creation. The move from Light to lights brings color and variety; so also does the move from Word (*logos*) to words. The shift to words does not invalidate the Word; it simply narrows the focus. As Tolkien wrote and as his mythology illustrates: "The λόγος is ultimately independent of the *verbum*" (*TLOT*, p. 269). As language proliferates and changes, reflecting the consciousness and world view of those who speak it, it reveals a spectrum of changing perception ranging from the light-infused Quenya of the High Elves of Valinor through the Sindarin of the Grey-elves of Middle-earth to the Black Speech of Mordor and the Orcs. It is just here that Tolkien's theory of sub-creation intersects Barfield's theory of the primal unity of meaning. The result is the nexus of myth and language, and a vivid illustration of how the latter is a "disease" of the former, arising out of an existing entity and yet affecting the growth of that entity by its presence.

Analysis of Tolkien's invented languages is necessarily limited to the little that has been published to date—phrases, songs, names, and epithets included in the books through their necessity to the plot and theme. In the words of editor Christopher Tolkien, the language notes appended to *The Silmarillion* are "necessarily very compressed, giving an air of certainty and finality that is not altogether justified; and they are very selective, this depending both on considerations of length and the limitations of the editor's knowledge" (*TS*, p. 355). The introduction to *Unfinished Tales* states that in cases where a story includes etymological material, it is primarily the narrative elements which have been extracted for publication.[1] In the acknowledged absence of complete data, it would be a serious error to attempt to demonstrate a completely coherent system of language. This *caveat* granted, however, we may with caution attempt to demonstrate a coherent concept behind the language, and use the available material to illustrate the concept.

Reflecting the presumed history of our own world, Tolkien gives language a relatively late entry into the history of Middle-earth. Long after creation and the wars of Melkor, the Firstborn of Ilúvatar, the elves, awaken in the starlit darkness by the lake Cuiviénen, the "Waters of Awakening." With their coming to consciousness, language begins, and with their language, their history begins. In any world this is an event of prime importance; in Tolkien's world we see it happen. Asleep, the elves are an unconscious part of creation.

---

[1] J.R.R. Tolkien, *Unfinished Tales of Númenor and Middle-earth*, ed. Christopher Tolkien (Boston: Houghton Mifflin, 1980), p. 10.

With their awakening they begin to perceive and interact with their surroundings. With and through the elves, their language, and their history, Tolkien makes real the interdependence of myth, language, and consciousness.

Elven language must derive from elven perception. When the elves awaken in the dark of Middle-earth, their first sight is the stars—* splintered light made by Varda against their coming. The result is speech. *"Ele!"*—an exclamation meaning "Behold!"—is the first utterance, "according," says the Appendix to *The Silmarillion*, "to Elvish legend" (*TS*, p. 358). Note here how reality is tied to perception, and the distinction between The Word and words made clear. The Word was the Music, made actual by the first imperative *"Eä!"* Both the Music and *Eä* precede and indeed determine elven perception. But "according to Elvish legend"—that is, from the elves' point of view, which is limited to their experience— *ele* is the first word.** It is their first perception and their agent of separation, dividing the see-ers from the seen, and

---

*Cf. Ernst Cassirer's *Language and Myth*, trans. Susanne K. Langer (New York: Harper and Brothers, 1946; rpt. New York: Dover Publications, 1953), p. 13. This work, first published in German as *Sprache und Mythos*, no. VI of *Studien der Bibliothek Warburg* (Leipzig: B.G. Teubner, 1925), cites a study of the Cora Indians, for whom "the first mythic impulse . . . was not toward making a sun-god or a lunar deity, but a community of stars." The likeness of this real tribe to Tolkien's fictional elves is too striking to pass without comment. Whether Tolkien was influenced by Cassirer or whether he reached independently toward the same image is of less importance than the fact that both were acknowledging an archetypal expression of myth-making consciousness. Cassirer's and Tolkien's work in this area began in the second and third decades of the twentieth century, a time when Jung was publishing on the idea of the collective unconscious. Mythic thinking was in the air.

**Tolkien's choice of *ele* as the first human utterance recalls Dante's deduction that the first word spoken by Adam must have been *El*, the name of God. Neither Tolkien's *ele* nor its derivative *el* functions in his language as a name for God. Nevertheless, both are names for first light, which (as in Tolkien's vision of the White Light) suggests God's emanation. The similarity of Tolkien's fictive first utterance to Dante's deduced one should not go unremarked. Cf. Howell's translation of the "De Vulgari Eloquentia" in *A Translation of The Latin Works of Dante Alighieri* (London: J.M. Dent, 1904), p. 12.

at the same time characterizing them by what they perceive and how they perceive it. *Ele* is a primary percept, but already we are on the way to metaphor, however gradual the road, as the elves take this perception into their lives, use it to shape their culture, splinter it, and re-diffuse it throughout their language.

The primal act of speech is response to light, to the percept "to shine," in exactly that primal wholeness which Barfield insists it must have had. It is the impulse behind elven language, giving it form and direction. More important, it gives the elves a sense of themselves as perceiving individuals. Light is the first observed phenomenon in their world, and reveals to them, in one way or another, all that they subsequently come to perceive. From the light-engendered act of speech comes their name for their language, Quenya, derived from *quen (quet)*, "say, speak." From the same base, *quen*, comes their first characterization of themselves. They are Quendi, "those that speak with voices," and this gives them their identity. Speech and the sense of self both come from the awareness of light. The names Quenya and Quendi establish the organizing principle of the elves' world and their language. Consciousness, expressed in speech, is relationship to light. In a very real sense, the elves are creating themselves in their own eyes, and this creation, like the initial creation by Eru and the Ainur, is governed by the interrelationship of light and word.

The elves name themselves Quendi out of their own inner impulse, but this is only the first of many names by which they are called. The Valar, beholding them, name them Eldar, "People of the Stars." By manifesting a need to link the elves with their first inspiration, this name suggests the separation between the two, and implies greater distance between the elves and the light than does their own name for themselves. But this name, too, derives in some degree from light and speech, since the first element, *el*, is clearly related to the primary *ele*. Subsequent differences in perception, arising from the continuing process of separation, lead to a variety of elven names. These names characterize the internal and external perceptions of different elven groups, and their relationships, both among themselves and to the light.

From the first utterance through a succession of elven names and concepts, the language is in a continuous process of fragmentation and modification. To fully appreciate this, we must re-examine the forces which operate in Tolkien's world, for language does not develop in a vacuum. It is the product of countervailing influences, of conflict leading to growth and separation leading to difference. The forces which shape elven language are partly external, impinging on the elves from without, and partly internal, involving their varying response to external circumstances and to each other.

Let us look first at the external forces. Elves, like the men who come after them, are exceptional in that they are the direct creation of Eru, and are no part of the creative labors of the Valar. "For the Children of Ilúvatar were conceived by him alone; and they came with the third theme, and were not in the theme which Ilúvatar propounded at the beginning, and none of the Ainur had part in their making" (TS, p. 18). Having no part in their creation, the Valar do not fully understand the elves, nor comprehend entirely what part they play in the unfolding history of the world. Again we must remind ourselves of the differing relationships that Eru and the Valar have with the world. Eru, having propounded the theme, knows and understands the Music. But he takes no further action, leaving the fulfillment of the Music to the Valar. While their task is to realize the Music, their knowledge of it is limited, since each knows only his own part, though it was sung in harmony with the others. They are the Powers of the World, but they do not fully know that world nor their own part in it. It follows that in Tolkien's complex, light-to-dark world, the actions of the Valar, however good their intent, do not always lead directly to good results.

Nowhere is this more clearly shown than in their decisions concerning the elves, decisions which directly affect the elven relationship to the light, which in turn changes and fragments their lives and their language. Recognizing and loving the elves as "things other than themselves," the Valar debate how best to guide them. A few favor leaving the elves free to live as they please in Middle-earth. Others, the majority, are afraid for the safety of the elves "in the dangerous world amid the deceits of the starlit dusk" (*TS*, p. 52). Unwilling, finally, to allow the elves to determine their own future, the Valar summon them to the safety of Valinor, to dwell in the light of the Trees. This would seem to have been an error in judgment, for "from this summons came many woes that afterwards befell" (*TS*, p. 52).

Among these "woes" must be counted the fragmentation and dispersion of the elven peoples, which contributes materially to the fragmentation and differentiation of their language. This is mythology in process, manifest by its "disease," language. Yet we must remember that all this has been foreshadowed and foresung in the Music, and must therefore ultimately derive from Eru. The separation gives rise to misunderstanding and alienation, but also to new perceptions and greater individuality. The "woes" are counterbalanced by new beauties, which otherwise would not have been. This seeming ambiguity in Tolkien's world, which allows for the building of "Gods and their houses out of dark and light," must be seen as addressing, if not yet solving, the polarity of light and dark, and justifying in large measure the tension between them.

These opposites—light and dark, good and evil—are always present and in operation, although often (and this may be deliberate on Tolkien's part) it is difficult to tell which is which. The summons to Valinor, intended to benefit the elves, has mixed results. It brings them into the bright light of the Trees, but forces decision on them rather than leaving them free. It complicates their relationship to the light, and in so doing also complicates their language. From these complications arise new differences. Where their first perception of the stars separated the elves from that which they beheld, these new differences separate elf from elf, word from word, and lead to the last splintering of the light itself as the process of separation continues and light and language fragment.

It is here that the internal forces which help to shape event and language come into play. In the first response to the summons of the Valar, three elven ambassadors, Ingwë, Finwë, and Elwë, go to Valinor to see for themselves the light of the Trees. Returning to Middle-earth, they urge the elves to answer the summons, but not all of the elves want to go. Thus the first separation occurs, dividing the elves into two peoples and eventually giving rise to two separate, though related, languages. The name Quendi, as describing a whole people, can no longer be used. The name Eldar, originally used to refer to all elves, now comes to be used only for those who go to Valinor. The name acquires a prefix—*tar*, "high"—and Tareldar, High Elves, are those who reach Valinor and dwell in its light. Those who do not go to Valinor are called the Avari, the Unwilling, the Refusers. In the course of time their language becomes differentiated from Quenya, reflecting their differences from the High Elves. The Avari are the elves who reject the light and choose to stay in Middle-earth, "preferring the starlight . . . to the rumour of the Trees" (*TS*, p. 52). They have no faith, unwilling as they are to predicate action on something they have not yet experienced. The difference which separates the believer from the unbeliever thus separates the High Elves from the Avari, and ultimately becomes the dividing line between light and dark. Fragmentation is beginning.

As the process continues, other names evolve to further characterize the division of the elves in their differing responses to the light. Those elves who go to Valinor acquire yet another name. They are Calaquendi, Elves of the Light. A clear symptom of the disease of mythology, the name is a modification of the original Quendi by the addition of *kal* or *cal*, "shine," and reflects the increasing need to use the language to make ever finer distinctions. It scarcely needs pointing out that it is also a perfect example of Barfield's unitary phrase "to shine" in the process of fragmenting from a "definite spiritual reality" to "pure human thinking" and "physical light." For "shine" is not a concept artibarily chosen and applied to the Calaquendi. Rather, it represents the need to express in words a more precise meaning, the shift of perception from a whole—Quendi—to a part of that whole which then becomes a new concept—Calaquendi. Stemming from the first sight of the stars, *quen,* "speak," came originally from the perception of "shine." Now only some speakers retain that concept, and the concept itself has intensified from the faint light of the stars to the bright light of the Trees. Moreover, this meaning can no longer be encompassed in the original word, but must be explained by another word.

And now the opposite concept—dark—enters the language. Those elves who stay in Middle-earth, themselves originally Quendi, come to be called Moriquendi, Elves of the Darkness. The word-forming process is the same as for Calaquendi, but the addition of *mor,* "dark," to the base noun is not simply a modification but a reversal of the original meaning. Here is fragmentation carried as far as it will go, the division of an original whole into opposite concepts, polarization reflected in words. Such a division clearly parallels the division of Eldar from Avari, since it relates to the same groups of people and occurs in response to the same event. This division, however, brings the language a little closer to metaphor, for light and dark can easily translate into enlightenment and ignorance, and the two words thus reflect a spiritual state in physical terms. What would be metaphor in our world is literal in Tolkien's, and yet manages to convey a metaphoric meaning as well. In addition, the name Moriquendi embodies a judgment, for it is what the Calaquendi call the Avari; it is not a name the Avari use of themselves. Thus it is clearly a comment made about one people by another. The original whole, Quendi, "those that speak with voices," is now divided by differences of perception and inclination.

Embedded in each name is a wealth of meaning relating word to phenomena and perception of phenomena, and further characterizing each group. "Those that speak with voices" spoke because they perceived the stars, fragments of light. *Calaquendi,* a refinement and intensification of *Quendi,* would literally mean "shine-speakers," or "light-speakers," and the Calaquendi would be those whose words conveyed light, revealed truth. *Moriquendi,* translated literally, would be "dark-speakers," "dark-sayers," those whose words express obscured perception. Here again, literality is on the way to metaphor. The Calaquendi see the light, a perception that is manifest in their speech. The Moriquendi do not see the light, and their language is darkened, obscuring their perception. To "see the light," in our world a figure of speech, a metaphor for an inner state, is in Tolkien's world an external reality relating to a historical event, while at the same time describing the ethos and cultural expressions of two different peoples.

While this division of Elves into groups labeled Light and Dark fits the reality of Tolkien's world, it is not his invention. The names and the concept, like many of the elements of Middle-earth, are borrowed from Norse mythology. Ljösalfar (light-elves) and döckalfar (dark-elves) are part of the world of the Norse *Prose Edda* and its earlier source, the *Poetic Edda*. Tolkien carries the concept beyond mere naming to establish a context in which light and dark occur, and to create a historical event by which the differences which underlie the distinction can be brought out and explained. Above all, it is language which gives to the concept its believability and solid reality. Elves of the Light and Elves of the Darkness, by their conflicting natures and related yet different modes of speech, build in Tolkien's world that "inner consistency of reality" which it is the function of language to give to any world.

Fragmentation of peoples, perception, and language follows a spasmodic and irregular course as the westward migration of the Calaquendi begins. A qualitative difference arising from willingness or unwillingness to see the light has divided what was originally a whole people, but the world of The Silmarillion is becoming a complex world, and the fragmentation will not stop with a simple division of light from dark, or follow a systematic or clearly defined pattern. Eventually there will be many shades and gradations of light among the peoples, with concomitant distinctions in language. The process, however, is fitful, with stops and starts, and changes both gradual and sudden.

The first change is one of degree, and, while it leads eventually to changes in language, it does not at first involve anything but relative promptness in response to the summons of the Valar. For those elves who choose to go to Valinor become separated by the degrees of eagerness with which they seek the light, and divide into three groups—the Vanyar (Fair Elves), the Noldor (Deep Elves), and the Teleri (Last-comers). As time passes, these divisions become more sharply drawn, until each group becomes an entity unto itself, defined by its differences from the others.

The three groups are led by those elven ambassadors who went first to Valinor to see the light. The Vanyar, led by Ingwë, are the first group to go. Their epithet, Fair Elves, refers directly to their golden hair, the only such coloring among the otherwise dark-haired elves. But it seems reasonable to suppose that both the epithet and the coloring are also meant to associate them with the light and with their readiness to seek it. These elves, once in Valinor, never leave it, but dwell always in the light. Perhaps because of their implied spirituality, they play little or no part in the subsequent turbulent history of the elves. Excitement and tension, after all, reside in opposition, in polarity, and there is neither opposition nor excitement in the sound of one hand clapping.

Next to go to Valinor are the Noldor, the Deep Elves, led by Finwë. A judgment is suggested here, for these elves are not fair, not quite so closely allied with the light. "Deep" is an epithet describing their nature as craftsmen and smiths, as makers. The name Noldor literally means "The Wise," from the stem ngol-, Quenya nolë, "long study, lore, knowledge." Here again a judgment is implied, for it is explained that the Noldor are "wise in the sense of possessing knowledge, not in the sense of possessing sagacity, sound judgment" (TS, p. 344). These characteristics of the Noldor are of key importance in Tolkien's history, and directly instrumental in the splintering of the light.

Last to go to Valinor are the Teleri, whose name is built on the stem tel-, "finish, end, be last." Led by Elwë, they are those who "were not wholly of a mind to pass from the dusk to the light of Valinor" (TS, p. 53). Not whole, divided in mind, the Teleri hesitate between light and dark. Although most of them eventually come to the light, some—and chief among these their leader, Elwë—turn aside and never reach Valinor. They are given yet another name, one which characterizes them not by what they are but by what they are not, a negative definition. They are Úmanyar, "those not of Aman." Aman, from *man*, "good, blessed, unmarred," is the Blessed Realm, Valinor, the home of the light. The introduction of *blessed* into the lexicon makes Tolkien's intention clear. The light and those who dwell in it are blessed, holy. Úman is unblessed, non-holy, for the *ú* prefix is plainly a negative. But *ú*, Úman equivalent to *un* in English, indicates negation, not opposition. It robs the attached word of its force but does not go so far as to make it mean the contrary. Thus Úmanyar, those who are not holy, stand in a neutral position with regard to the light.

These subdivisions, interesting in themselves, give rise to more and narrower concepts in the language, while the two major divisions still stand. The Fair Elves, the Deep Elves, and the Last-comers, already differentiated from one another in character, are still Eldar, or Tareldar, High Elves. They are all Calaquendi, all Elves of the Light. "Fair," "Deep," and "Last" are not opposing terms, but suggest distinct differences among peoples. The others, Úmanyar and Avari, are Moriquendi, Elves of the Darkness, but within this blanket term they are distinguished from one another by differing attitudes toward the light and degrees of readiness to seek it. Those who refuse the light altogether are not quite the same as those who are willing to seek it but allow themselves to become diverted. Within the developing polarities of light and dark among the elven peoples, degrees of intensity begin to sketch in the force field between the positive and negative poles of the Secondary World. In the ensuing history we will hear very little of the Vanyar or of the Avari. It is the interaction and clash of the Noldor, the Teleri, and the Úmanyar which will generate action and give rise to the song and story of The Silmarillion.

The polarities and the force field are reflected in the language. We have seen that the very act of speech comes from light: the language is formed and informed by that awareness of light with which the elves came to consciousness. And as language develops, as the elves begin to coalesce into discrete groups, the language shows a concomitant awareness of degrees and kinds of light, and of the shading which leads to light's opposite, darkness. The concept of "to shine" breaks up into kinds of shining, into "gleam," "sparkle," "radiant." Color-words appear—green, gold, silver, grey. And darker words appear, words for dusk, dimness, twilight, shadow. Light diminished, darkness illumined, throw one another into relief, for light and dark, like all polar contrarieties, exist not only at each other's expense but also by virtue of each other. Only in full knowledge of one is it possible to fully know the other.

As time passes after the division of the elves into Cala-quendi and Moriquendi, the language itself begins to divide. A second language, Sindarin, evolves. Although the evolution and the separation from Quenya take time, the existence of this second language is a direct result of the summons to Valinor. Sindarin is spoken by the elves of Middle-earth, while Quenya comes to be spoken only in Valinor by those elves who dwell in the light. Degree of proximity to light thus affects the semantic, morphological, and phonological char-acteristics of each language. The same lessened perception of light that divides Moriquendi from Calaquendi distinguishes Sindarin from Quenya.

Before embarking on any analysis of the differences be-tween Tolkien's two main invented languages, we must ac-knowledge that these differences exist on two levels—one real and one fictional. At the real level they are simply the differences between Finnish, the model for Quenya, and Welsh, the model for Sindarin. At this level the differences are sim-ply a function of Tolkien's own preferences; he liked the shape and sound of words in both languages. The fictional level, however, is the important one, both in its support of the reality of the fictional world and in an exploration of its relation to Barfield's theory. For at the fictional level each language must express the people who speak it, and must also be their sub-creative instrument for making a world.

We must also be aware that, as is the case with Tolkien's languages in general, much of the data necessary to explore differences is unavailable. We do not have all the words, and those we do have are not always marked either Quenya or Sindarin. Some knowledge of Tolkien's method, however, and the general principles by which he worked will give us ground on which to base a tentative examination of relationships between Quenya and Sindarin. A helpful account of Tolkien's working method is given by Humphrey Carpenter:

> Besides Quenya and Sindarin, Tolkien invented a number of other elvish languages. Though these existed only in outline, the complexities of their interrelationship and the elaboration of a "family tree" of languages occupied much of his mind. But the elvish names in *The Silmarillion* were constructed almost exclusively from Quenya and Sindarin.
>
> It is impossible in a few sentences to give an adequate account of how Tolkien used his elvish languages to make names for the characters and places in his stories. But briefly, what happened was this. When working to plan he would form all these names with great care, first deciding on the meaning, and then developing its form first in one language and subsequently in the other; the form finally used was most frequently that in Sindarin. (*TAB*, p. 94)

The idea of a "family tree" of languages, much like the family of Indo-European languages in our world, clearly suggests related languages differentiated by varying circumstances of geography and culture, circumstances which we have already seen at work in the world of The Silmarillion. And just as ancient and modern European languages can lead back to the hypothetical, reconstructed Indo-European, our putative earliest language, so both Quenya and Sindarin are presumed to derive from a "primitive Eldarin" no longer spoken. That Tolkien more frequently used the Sindarin form of a word reflects the fact that in his fictional world Sindarin was more widely used than Quenya.

The path of light can be clearly traced in Tolkien's languages. From the primal *ele* comes what Tolkien calls "the ancient element *El*, 'star,' in Q. *elen*, S. *el*."[2] From these are

---

[2] J.R.R. Tolkien, *The Road Goes Ever On: A Song Cycle*, poems by J.R.R. Tolkien set to music by Donald Swann (Boston: Houghton Mifflin, 1967), p. 65.

derived the adjectival forms *elena* and *elda*, "of the stars." The plural of *elda* is *eldar*, which, with its variant *eldalië*, becomes the generic name of the elves. The singular form undergoes a semantic shift from "star" to "elf" in Quenya *elda*, Sindarin *edhel*, a shift which indicates the importance of the light/star concept to elven identity. The *êl* morpheme has thus come full circle, for it first marked an act of perception—"behold"—which distinguished a people from what they perceived. It then became a concept—"star"—defining that which they recognized as separate from themselves. It now becomes the word—*elf*—through which they identify themselves in terms of what they see.

Following this line of development, *êl* becomes the basis for a number of elven names, all of them carrying the reference "star" with the embedded meaning "light." The name Elbereth is a good example. Readers of *The Lord of the Rings* will recognize Elbereth as a name invoked in times of danger, having by its very sound the power to drive away evil. Sung by Gildor and the elves in the woods of the Shire, it drives off the Black Rider who had been pursuing Frodo and his companions. Similarly, in the battle at Weathertop, Frodo's cry " 'O Elbereth! Gilthoniel!' " drives off the King of the Ringwraiths. Aragorn, examining the knife with which Frodo struck at his enemy, comments, " 'More deadly to him was the name of Elbereth' " (*LOTR*, I, p. 265). And Sam calls on Elbereth when he and Frodo are escaping from the Tower of Cirith Ungol, an invocation that breaks the evil power of the Watchers.

Elbereth is the Sindarin form of an elven name for Varda, the Queen of the Valar. More than any other being in The Silmarillion, she is associated with light in both its physical and spiritual aspects. She kindled the Lamps and made stars from the dew of Telperion, the silver Tree. In one of the few statements directly connecting light with Eru, Varda is described as having "the light of Ilúvatar" in her face. And we are told that "in light is her power and her joy" (*TS*, p. 26). As bringer of light she is bringer of vision and perception, for it is said of her spouse Manwë, King of the Valar, that when he looks out from his throne, "if Varda is beside him, he sees further than all other eyes" (*TS*, p. 26).

All of this meaning is embedded in her Sindarin name, Elbereth, and its Quenya equivalent, Elentári. Quenya *elen* and Sindarin *êl* both carry the primal "star" meaning. The Quenya suffix *tar*, "high," in its feminine form *tári* ("high," therefore "queen"), when attached to *elen* gives us "Star-Queen," by implication "Queen of Light." The more frequently used Sindarin form, Elbereth, is also translated "Star-Queen," but analysis shows it to have a different meaning, typical of the diminution of perception from Quenya to Sindarin. The "star" element is retained in the first syllable, *el*, but the second element, *bereth*, literally means "spouse," and means queen only by extension, as "spouse of a king." The shift from *tári* to *bereth* is thus in a sense a demotion. The Quenya name recognizes Varda as queen in her own right, suggesting the elevated feminine principle as bringer of light, whereas the Sindarin name emphasizes first her role as wife, and only secondarily as queen.

Elentári and Elbereth are epithets characterizing Varda as she is perceived by the Calaquendi and Moriquendi respectively. They are thus not true names. But a number of elves have names which carry the "star" component. From *êl* comes Elrond (Star-dome), Elros (Star-foam), Elwing (Star-spray), and Elwë (The Star). The element *wë* is not translated, but occurs frequently as a suffix, and is probably an enclitic article, "the" or "a." From Sindarin *edhel* comes the name Aredhel (Noble Elf), and from the variant form *eledh* comes Eledhwen (Star-maiden). From Quenya *elen* comes Elendil, with the combined meanings "Star-lover" and "Elf-friend." Also from *elen* come the names Elenwë (The Star), Elenmirë (Star-jewel), and Elenna (Starwards), originally a directional term which becomes the elven name for Númenor.

The star/light concept proliferates as language develops. Its continuance can be traced semantically, phonologically, and morphologically. Semantically derived from *êl* is the phonologically and morphologically similar noun *ril*, "brilliance." Added to the stem *ita-*, "sparkle," this gives the Quenya name Itarillë or Itarildë, "Sparkling Brilliance," which shortens in Sindarin to Idril. This name is of almost religious significance in elven history, for Idril is the elven princess who marries Tuor, a mortal man, and gives birth to the savior figure Eärendil. The phonologically separate but semantically linked stem *tin-*, "sparkle," is found in Quenya *tinwë*, "spark," *tintilar*, "to sparkle, glitter," and *tinta*, "cause to sparkle." It combines with Quenya *dōmē* to form *tindómë*, "starry twilight," from which comes *tindómerel*, "daughter of twilight," Tinúviel in Sindarin. This last is another key name in elven history, for Tinúviel is the epithet given by Beren to Lúthien, an elven princess closely and curiously connected with the light (her story, a significant one, will be examined later). *Tin-* is also the basis for another Quenya epithet for Varda— Tintallë, The Kindler, "She that causes sparkling, kindles lights."

Quenya *kal-*, *cal-* (Sindarin *gal-*) and Quenya *sil-* (Sindarin *thil-*) are phonologically and morphologically developed from *êl*. Both mean "shine," *kal-* in a general sense, *sil-* more narrowly, as "shine with white or silver light." *Kal-* appears in the already-cited Calaquendi, in *calen*, "green" (glossed as "etymologically 'bright' "), and in slightly altered form in Quenya *alkar*, *alcar*, from which comes Alcarinquë (The Glorious), a name for one of Varda's stars. The Sindarin form is *aglar*, which occurs in Aglarond, the Glittering Caverns which so bewitch the dwarf Gimli at the battle of Helm's Deep. Extended forms of *kal-* and *gal-* appear in Quenya Al(a)táriël, Sindarin Galadriel, which means "Maiden crowned with a radiant garland." It occurs also in the Sindarin Gil-galad, "Radiant Star" or "Star of Bright Light." The element *gil* in this last name is a Sindarin word which literally means "bright spark," but which, like Quenya *tinwë*, "spark," was often used in the sense of "star." It appears also in Sindarin Gilthoniel, an epithet for Varda which is almost never used alone but always in conjunction with Elbereth, as in Frodo's cry, " 'O Elbereth! Gilthoniel!' " Gilthoniel is translated "Star-Kindler," and thus parallels Quenya Tintallë, "The Kindler." A significant difference in the construction of the two names is the Sindarin addition of *gil* to *thoniel*, "kindler," a refinement of the whole meaning encompassed by the Quenya word. Where Quenya Tintallë is simply *tinta* plus what appears to be an agentive suffix, thus "Kindler," literally "sparkle-er" and colloquially "Star-er," the Sindarin must be more specific and, in effect, say the same thing twice to ensure precision of meaning.

The modification of language from Quenya to Sindarin is an index of the greater sense of separation from light felt by the elves of Middle-earth. Quenya takes its name from the word for light-inspired speech. Sindarin, in contrast, is formed from Quenya *sinda*, "grey," a word which itself expresses diminished light. While it eventually becomes the principal language of Middle-earth, the first to use this second language are the Sindar, the Grey-elves, called Elves of the Twilight. This is a new name and a new shade in Tolkien's spectrum. Grey is a middle shade, twilight a midpoint between daylight and dark. Like their name, the Sindar are in the middle-range— between Calaquendi and Moriquendi, between enlightenment and ignorance. This would seem to suggest—and Tolkien's development of plot and character supports the idea— that the Sindar can go either way. Theirs is not just a case of seeking and seeing the light or rejecting it outright. Theirs is a world in which even those who have not seen the light can, if they wish, be aware of it, and know its power.

Since they are of the elves who stay in Middle-earth and never go to Valinor, the Sindar should be counted among the Moriquendi. They are distinct from the Dark Elves, however, set apart by the special relationship to light enjoyed by their king, Elu Thingol, and his queen, Melian. Of all the Sindar, only these two have actually seen the light. Of the two, Melian is the greater: she is a Maia, one of the lesser Valar, and thus has lived in the light of the Trees. Like Yavanna, she is a singer of songs, and like Varda, she is a bringer of light. Coming to Middle-earth at the time of the awakening of the elves, she fills the pre-dawn darkness with singing, and has "the light of Aman" in her face (*TS*, p. 55). The association with light and song puts Melian very near the Valar and very close to the primacy of creation. Nevertheless, there are some differences. The comparisons with Yavanna and Varda are deliberate, intended to show similarities but also to point up distinctions between them and Melian. Her singing has not that power which, in Yavanna's singing, created the two Trees. Nor is "the light of Aman" in her face that direct and primary "light of Ilúvatar" which illumines the face of Varda. Close to the light, given the gift of song, Melian is yet a slight diminution. The light she brings to the Sindar is more than they have had, less than they might have had. It is the middle ground of their possible choices.

Unlike Melian, Thingol has not dwelt in the light, but he has seen it and directly experienced it. He was that Elwë who, with Finwë and Ingwë, went as an ambassador to Valinor. He and Olwë, his brother, led the Teleri, the Last-comers, on their long journey toward the light. That fact in itself tells us something, for having seen the light, Elwë is still the last to take his people to Valinor. Moreover, he voluntarily gives up his opportunity to see the light again, for although he "desired greatly the light and splendour of the Trees" (*TS*, p. 52), he does not return to Valinor, but chooses to stay in Middle-earth. In the course of his journey toward the light, Elwë meets Melian in Nan Elmoth, the aptly named Valley of Star-dusk, and falls in love with her. Forgetting his journey, he stays with her in a trance of love "while long years were measured by the wheeling stars above them" (*TS*, p. 55). Though they search for a while for their lost leader, most of the Teleri eventually continue without him. While they complete their journey, he does not. He forgets his desire for the light, content to stay in the darkness of Middle-earth.

Yet he has light of a kind. "Greatly though he had desired to see again the light of the Trees, in the face of Melian he beheld the light of Aman as in an unclouded mirror, and in that light he was content" (*TS*, p. 58). Tolkien's emphasis on the light as seen in the face of the beloved is perhaps a reference to the medieval concept of earthly love as the reflection of divine love. Elwë's love for Melian takes him as near the divine as any earthly lover can come in mortal love, for Tolkien makes it clear that she represents light. Still, she herself is not the source of it: while the mirror is "unclouded," the light is still once removed from its source, reflected light. Yet such light is undeniably better than no light at all. A secondary, diminished light, it still conveys the reflection of the primary value.

Elwë himself suggests diminished light through the etymology of his name. His Quenya name is Elwë Singollo, Elwë Greymantle. As we have seen, his first name is simply *êl*, "star," plus the article *wë*. His second name, while it does not negate the implied light of his first name, has the effect of muting it. Singollo is formed from Quenya *sinda*, "grey," plus *collo*, "cloak," with the hard *c* of the second element lenited by its position between vowels to hard *g*, and the last syllable of *sinda* dropped. The juxtaposition of "Star" and "Greymantle" implies light dimmed, an initial brightness cloaked or mantled over. The name thus prefigures Elwë's choice of Middle-earth and reflected light over Aman and the light of the Trees. And with this choice comes a change in his name, a change which further suggests his dimmed luster. His Sindarin name is Elu, not Elwë. The *wë* suffix contracts and darkens to *u*, which may carry the same negative force found in the *ú* prefix of Úmanyar. In another change, Singollo modifies to Thingol, the *s* softened to unvoiced *th*, and the last syllable gone completely. Both semantically and phonologically his name is dimmed, softened. He is diminished light.

The change in Thingol's name is typical of the sound shifts that occur as light-infused Quenya modifies to twilight Sindarin. In related words marked as Quenya or Sindarin the shift appears to follow a pattern of softening, most clearly perceptible in consonants. Thus medial *d* in Quenya *elda* goes to *dh* with the value of voiced English *th* in Sindarin *edhel*. Initial *k* or *c*, as in Quenya *kal*, *cal*, becomes hard *g*, as in Sindarin *gal*. Initial *s* in Quenya *sil* softens to unvoiced *th* in Sindarin *thil*. We have already seen that Quenya *sinda* becomes Sindarin *thin*. I will not attempt an extensive comparison of Quenya and Sindarin; that must wait until there is much more data to go on than is now available. But I do want to show, briefly, a correlation between what happens to light and what happens to language in Tolkien's mythology. All of the words cited above are light-related, and all of them become softened in the shift from Quenya to Sindarin. It can be no accident.

Qualitatively, the shift gives Sindarin its own individuality and its own beauty, different from but no less appealing than Quenya. In her handbook on the languages of Middle-earth, Ruth Noel cites the concluson of a linguist from San Diego State University, Dr. Thomas Donahue, that Sindarin is "more elegant and melodic" than Quenya.[3] But each language has value for those who speak it, and we must be careful not to turn observations of sound shifts into qualitative judgments, or to assume because of the differences beween them that Quenya is "good" and Sindarin is "bad," or even that Quenya is good and Sindarin is less good. Sindarin is farther from the light, but closer to the activities and concerns of Middle-earth.

If this seems like a paradox, it is only one of many in the work of a most paradoxical man, "a man of antitheses," whose work is built on paradox and polarity. Tolkien thought of the development of language as the proper activity of the mind of man. In his work we find no implication that he conceived of language as deteriorating from an earlier and better to a later and worse state as it developed. Rather, we must conclude on the basis of his knowledge of and love for the numerous ancient and modern languages which he spoke and read that he saw language as beautiful in its variety, and as inevitably proliferating and changing as the perceptions of mankind proliferate and change. In his mythology he envisioned that proliferation and change as consonant with the splintering of the light.

Tolkien loved the power latent in language—that "mythical grammar" by which man can, through his perception and invention, sub-create and make a Secondary World. To hear or to speak a strange language is to be for the moment in a new and strange world created by different perception and a different imaginative vision. This is, in effect, a Secondary

---

[3]Ruth S. Noel, *The Languages of Tolkien's Middle-earth* (Boston: Houghton Mifflin, 1980), p. 72.

World which we see refracted through the prism of language. We may say, then, that *any* world in which man lives and speaks is sub-created by him, and is thus a Secondary World, in that he cannot see directly what God spoke and made in the Logos, but only what man speaks and makes with splintered light. The separation of man from God is tragic, and the splintering of light and language is the result of the Fall. But Tolkien surely felt, with Augustine, the possibilities for beauty that derived from the *felix peccatum Adae*, the fortunate sin of Adam. Given light and language, it is man's right to make by that law wherein he is made, and through that making to "assist in the effoliation and multiple enrichment of creation." And Tolkien just as surely felt, with Barfield, that in the hands of the poets, the makers, that "disease of mythology" called language will be the instrument whereby sub-creation will re-unite word and percept, and re-unite man with God.

> All tales may come true; and yet, at the last, redeemed, they may be as like and as unlike the forms that we give them as Man, finally redeemed, will be like and unlike the fallen that we know.

V
LIGHT INTO DARKNESS

Nothing is evil in the beginning.

TOLKIEN, THE FELLOWSHIP OF THE RING

Modification and proliferation of language, fragmentation of perception and meaning, division and sub-division of the elven race—all these are manifestations of that splintering which Tolkien sees as the fate of the White Light refracted. But what of the light itself? By Tolkien's own standard for sub-creation, light should manifest the same splintering if his Secondary World is to have the inner consistency of reality. And indeed it does. Division and sub-division of light parallel these same patterns in Tolkien's world and his languages. Moreover, his treatment of light lends itself increasingly to the working-out of Barfield's division of "to shine" into spiritual reality and physical light, a division which leads to metaphor and symbol. Tolkien has devised for his light a pattern of diminution and fragmentation leading to its increasing spiritual and physical distance from the inhabitants of Middle-earth. This pattern begins with the pervasive light of the Lamps, continues with the softer, cyclical light of the Trees, and culminates in the Silmarils, the three great jewels which hold the last light of the destroyed Trees. Their resting-places, the "long home" of each in earth, sea, and sky, put the light beyond the reach of Middle-earth. The last of the light, the star Eärendil, which is the only remaining Silmaril, appears to Middle-earth at morning and evening, times of changing light. No longer a pervasive presence, the light has become only a reminder and a promise, a sign of what has been and yet may be.

This final splintering of the light is the result of the last great act of sub-creation. Out of the mingled light of the two Trees, Fëanor, the great Noldoran smith, creates the Silmarils. These jewels then become the focus for all the impulses, desires, and conflicting emotions which Tolkien sees as responses to light. At the same time they function as the prism for the refraction and dispersal of those responses throughout the life of Middle-earth and its peoples. They are the nexus to which everything that has gone before points, out of which everything which comes after flows. Light and dark, positive and negative, good and ill—all the polarities come together in the effects of the Silmarils, the last splinters of the light.

To see this in perspective, we must backtrack a little and examine the separate characteristics of the three elven kindreds who go to Valinor. In particular we must look at the Noldor. The Noldor, you remember, are the middle group of the Calaquendi, those who respond to the summons of the Valar and seek the light. All three kindreds are important, however, for Tolkien has assigned a special value to each. Taken together, the three are a paradigm of the spectrum of human spirituality and response to God.

The first to go, the smallest group and the most select in terms of their affinity for light, are the Vanyar. Golden-haired, Fair Elves, they dwell in the light ever after their arrival in Valinor. There they come under the special guardianship of Manwë and Varda, the highest of the Valar. (Relationships between elves and Valar are significant, for they embody much of Tolkien's underlying philosophical and theological theme.) The special provinces of Manwë and Varda are respectively air and light. Varda, Queen of stars and light, kindled the Lamps and made newer and brighter stars for the coming of the elves. Manwë Súlimo, "The Breather," is Lord of Arda, the earth, and his presence is manifest in its airs and winds. (It scarcely needs pointing out here that underlying the concept of Manwë is the whole spirit-breath-wind triad that Barfield used to illustrate primal unity of meaning.) Thus air and light, the most spiritual, least material of the earth's elements, are associated by extension with the Vanyar.

At the opposite end of the spectrum are the Teleri. They are the last to go to Valinor, the least eager for the light, and (in sad commentary on humankind) the largest group. Like the majority of humanity, the Teleri vacillate, hesitate, and are changeful in mind and spirit. This changefulness is exemplified in the two figures Tolkien chose to guide the Teleri: Ulmo, the Vala whose province is water, and his vassal, the Maia Ossë. The association of the Teleri with water says much, for in Tolkien's mythology, water, more than any other substance of Middle-earth, has in it the echo of the Music.* In the world's mythologies, water is used to suggest creation, death, and rebirth, and Tolkien is building on its real mythic and psychological value. But by investing the waters of Middle-earth with the echo of the Music, Tolkien has used the very nature of the element to embody the strife, the beauty, and the contention of his creation myth. In water there is music, but there is also storm; waves and currents keep water always in motion, always mutable. All this is embodied in the Teleri. Their name for themselves is Lindar, the Singers. They love water, and always live near the sea, on the shores of both Valinor and Middle-earth. But they are poised between Ulmo, lord of the deeps and oceans, and Ossë, who rules the coasts and islands and delights in storms. Ulmo and Ossë do not always agree, and when Ulmo leads the Teleri to the shores of Aman, Ossë persuades some of them to remain on the shores of Middle-earth. Thus the Teleri are marginal, both literally and metaphorically.

Between the extremes, between those most eager for light and those least eager, are the Noldor. Because they are in the center, equidistant between poles, they are central to Tolkien's concept and to the theme and action of The Silmarillion.

The Noldor, as Tolkien represents them, embody the

---

*"And it is said by the Eldar that in water there lives yet the echo of the Music of the Ainur more than in any substance else that is in this Earth; and many of the Children of Ilúvatar hearken still unsated to the voices of the Sea, and yet know not for what they listen" (TS, p. 19). Tolkien's explicit linking of the Sea with the Music of creation clarifies the episode mentioned in Chapter II concerning Frodo's dream of the tower and the sea. Unknowing, Frodo is responding to the Music. While this cannot explain Tolkien's use of the same image in his Beowulf allegory on a logical basis, it may illuminate it on a psychological basis, in that Tolkien's own perception of the sea informs both his reading of Beowulf and his writing of The Silmarillion.

highest level of humanity's achievement and potential. Of all the Three Kindreds, they make the most material contributions to art and science, to what we think of as civilization. They are the makers, the smiths, the craftsmen. As such, they are beloved of Aulë, the Maker-Vala whose special province is the fabric of the earth. In one respect Aulë is the most human of the Valar, for he is the only one of them who has the impulse to imitate his maker by creating a race of people. In making the dwarves he exceeds his mandate (as man the maker has a tendency to do) and is rebuked by Eru. His defense is a re-statement of the line from "Mythopoeia" that "we make still by that law wherein we're made," for he replies to Eru: " 'Yet the making of things is in my heart from my own making by thee; and the child of little understanding that makes a play of the deeds of his father may do so without thought of mockery, but because he is the son of his father' " (*TS*, p. 43). Aulë's humble acceptance of Eru's chastisement and his offer to destroy his creatures recalls the unquestioning obedience of Abraham and his willingness to sacrifice his son at God's command.

The association of the Noldor with Aulë is surely part of Tolkien's intent to remind us of humanity's great potential to excel, but also to exceed. The characteristics of the Noldor—ability to create, potential to excel, tendency to exceed the limits—raise questions about the nature of the connection between obedience and freedom, and provide a vivid illustration of the relationship between man and God as Tolkien sees it. For while the Noldor share Aulë's creativity and skill and his desire to make, they do not have his readiness to submit to a higher will, nor that absence of desire which keeps him free of his possessions. For "the delight and pride of Aulë is in the deed of making, and in the thing made, and neither in possession nor in his own mastery" (*TS*, p. 19). But the Noldor cannot loose themselves from their possessions nor from their pride in their making. The greatness of the Noldor, which is also the flaw which leads them to rebellion and disaster, is embodied in their name. They are "The Wise," yet only "wise in the sense of possessing knowledge, not in the sense of possessing sagacity, sound judgment."

Tolkien's characterization of the Noldor might well stand as a historian's description of any of the great civilization-builders of past ages, and is a clear characterization of our own Western, post-Renaissance culture:

> Great became their knowledge and their skill; yet even greater was their thirst for more knowledge, and in many things they soon surpassed their teachers. They were changeful in speech, for they had great love of words, and sought ever to find names more fit for all things that they knew or imagined. (*TS*, p. 60)

And further:

> . . . the Noldor advanced ever in skill and knowledge; and the long years were filled with their joyful labours, in which many new things fair and wonderful were devised. Then it was that the Noldor first bethought them of letters, and Rúmil of Tirion was the name of the loremaster who first achieved fitting signs for the recording of speech and song, some for graving upon metal or in stone, others for drawing with brush or with pen. (*TS*, p. 63)

Here is quintessential humanity, seeking knowledge, devising new things, developing language, inventing writing, above all making always newer and more precise names for things, moving from percept to concept in refinement of verbal expression. In their skill and eagerness to make and name, they perforce divide the whole into more and more parts, and those parts into ever more discrete units. This same division occurs in their making of letters and devising of script, for the written word fixes and preserves the name yet separates it even farther from the thing it names. Concept, then, becomes entirely independent of percept—indeed, becomes a thing in itself, transmittable through signs which do not even need the associated sound.

This is the work of the Noldor, and of all the Noldor the greatest, the most gifted, the most powerful, and therefore the one with the greatest potential for good or ill, is Fëanor, the son of Finwë. If the Noldor are the quintessence of humanity, Fëanor is the quintessence of the Noldor; in him all their characteristics are magnified, all their virtues and flaws increased tenfold. Fëanor is crown prince of the Noldor, the only child of the marriage of Finwë and Míriel, and his birth is portentous for the fates of elves and of Middle-earth. The time of his birth is described as a time of glory and bliss in Valinor, a time when participation in the light of the Trees is at its peak. With telling choice of words Tolkien describes this time as "the Noontide of the Blessed Realm," its time of brightest light, the high point between rising and setting which is also the moment when the light begins to decline, when the turn toward dark begins. This is implicit in the birth of Fëanor, as it is explicit in his later deeds and acts. Míriel, his mother, worn out in bearing him, yearns for "release from the labour of living" (*TS*, p. 63). She chooses to die, thus going against her elven fate, which is to live while the world exists. Her death leaves the headstrong Fëanor motherless and leads to the marriage of Finwë and Indis, a Vanya, and to the birth of their two sons, Fingolfin and Finarfin. Dissension between Fëanor and his half-brothers leads to the Exile of the Noldor from Aman and their long travail in Middle-earth.

The death of Míriel has profound consequences which stem directly from the unchecked nature of Fëanor. He embodies all the desire to achieve, all the skill and knowledge, all the potential for good and ill of the Noldor. His true name is Curufinwë, by the addition of *curu*, "skill," to his father's name. It is Míriel who first calls him Fëanor, "Spirit of Fire," a name made by combining *fëa*, "spirit," with the genitive of *nar*, "fire." By this name he is characterized and by this name he is always known, but the fact that it is an epithet and not a true name is significant, for it suggests an emphasis upon one element of his nature to the exclusion of all others.

The appearance of fire at the noontide of the light signals a qualitative change in the potential course of events. In addition, Fëanor's appearance among the Noldor is paralleled by the re-appearance of Melkor among the Valar. Melkor has been re-instated after long banishment, a forgiveness which implies hope for his true repentance and reform. For both

Fëanor and Melkor to appear at this time suggests the precarious perfection of the moment, wherein the peak of brightness is also the most delicate point of balance. Light and concepts derived from light have been the guiding force of the history so far: truth, illumination, enlightenment, together with their opposites—obscurity, darkness, ignorance, dimmed perception. Fire brings a new force to bear, for it is heat as well as light, hottest where it is brightest. Fire shares with its opposite, water, the semblance of life independent of any force but its own. Fire is, in fact, more closely associated with humanity than is light, and has in itself an immediate potential to help or to harm, to warm or to consume. Comparison with the myth of Prometheus is tempting here, nor is it wholly irrelevant, for Fëanor is a Promethean figure in Tolkien's mythology. Without trying to make one-to-one correspondences, we can still see in both stories the theme of the overreacher whose excess is punished, yet whose accomplishments succeed in bringing humanity a spark which can elevate humankind above its condition and carry it forward.

Fëanor's associations with fire in all their negative and positive connotations begin immediately with the description of Míriel's bearing of him, in which she is "consumed in spirit and body" (*TS*, p. 63). His spirit burns "as a flame" (*TS*, p. 60). His hands and mind are seldom at rest; he has a quickness, a leaping, flickering restlessness of flame reminiscent of Loge in Wagner's *Nibelungenlied.* He is "driven by the fire of his own heart only, working ever swiftly and alone" (*TS*, p. 66).

As a maker Fëanor surpasses all of his kindred. He is "of all the Noldor, then or after, the most subtle in mind and the most skilled in hand" (*TS*, p. 64). Improving on the letters of Rúmil, he devises the Fëanorian script, a beautification and refinement which makes writing, an instrument for the division of meaning, into an artifact, a thing beautiful in itself apart from any meaning. Fëanor also makes jewels. The Noldor have always excelled at this, digging gemstones from the earth and cutting and carving them into many shapes. But Fëanor goes beyond them, for he discovers "how gems greater and brighter than those of the Earth might be made with skill" (*TS,* p. 64). In this he approaches Aulë, who has made the gems of the earth.

The words which Tolkien chooses to apply to Fëanor are worth noting, for, as always, Tolkien means what he says, and uses each word for all the resonance inherent in it. *Subtle* and *skilled* are words repeatedly coupled with Fëanor's name. Anyone familiar with the third chapter of Genesis will at once remember the description of the serpent as "the most subtle of the beasts of the field," and will consequently be alive to the negative connotations of the word and to the barely hinted association of Fëanor with the serpent. The word itself has several meanings. We may safely dispense with the first dictionary definition of "slight, not immediately obvious," since it clearly does not apply to Fëanor, who is anything but slight in either stature or impact. The second and third definitions, however, do reveal him, and make it clear that Tolkien is using the word for all the force it has. "Able to make fine distinctions, keen" and "characterized by skill or ingenuity, clever"—both of these definitions describe Fëanor as he is first seen by the reader. But further definitions—"characterized by craft or slyness, devious" and "operating in a hidden and usually injurious way; insidious"— point to developments in Fëanor's character which the reader can clearly see taking place over the course of time. *Subtle* can be traced back to Indo-European *teks-,* "to weave; also to fabricate," from which it develops through the suffixed form *teks-la* to Latin *tela,* "warp," and thence to *sub-tela,* "thread passing under the warp." So the character of Fëanor, son of Míriel the weaver, runs crosswise to the thread of life in Aman, becoming part of the fabric but at right angles to its direction.

Skill yields an equal wealth of meaning for our knowledge of Fëanor. It can be traced back to Indo-European *skel-,* "to cut," and thus suggests that tendency to divide and separate which is characteristic of the Noldor. We have already seen it at work in the larger context of the development of language and culture. *Skel-* is related to Old Norse *skil,* "reason, discernment, knowledge," and thus suggests that means of knowing through analysis, through the making of distinctions among things and ideas, which is the distinguishing characteristic of the scientific method and also of that creation of post-Renaissance man, the Age of Reason.

The creation of the Silmarils is the greatest of all Fëanor's great works. We are told that he summoned "all his lore, and his power [potency, potential], and his subtle skill; and at the end of all he made the Silmarils" (TS, p. 67). The Silmarils, focus of much of the conflict and controversy which mark Tolkien's history, lend themselves to uses both dramatic and thematic. They function as literal artifacts, as potent metaphors, and at the highest level as symbols charged with referents. Consonant with the actual fragmentation of light is fragmentation of meaning, and the division of meaning into literal, metaphoric, and symbolic levels. It is a measure of Tolkien's creativity and the wholeness of his concept that he has achieved this at no cost to the reality of his world or the believability of its history. The Silmarils are literal reality, metaphor, and symbol without ever being anything other than themselves.

As artifacts the Silmarils embody light as a physical reality which can be worked like matter, touched and handled. As jewels they are a metaphor for both the desire of all mankind to possess beauty and for the negative of this desire: covetousness, lust, and selfishness. Since it is enclosed in jewels, the light of the Silmarils, unlike that of the Trees from which it comes, does not necessarily shine for all and on all. It can be possessed by one individual, held in the hand, worn, or hidden away at the owner's whim. While Fëanor's motive in making the Silmarils is to preserve the light, his choice of jewels as bodies for that light leads to misunderstanding and misuse.

While their actuality leads to the dramatic action of the history, and their metaphoric value enriches Tolkien's meaning, it is as symbols that the Silmarils work most powerfully. In this regard they are the embodiment of Tolkien's theme of the power of light. Through the Silmarils he makes his clearest statement about the need for light, the impulse to seek it, and the perversion of that impulse into lust and hatred as desire turns in on itself and possession masters the possessor. The story becomes an exploration of the various effects of light and the terrible way in which the light, wholly good in itself, can yet lead into darkness and even, in the ultimate inversion of its quality, can become that darkness.

The relationship between Fëanor and the Silmarils is a close one, not only because he makes and cherishes them but because each is a kind of likeness, a reversed image of the other. Each is unique, not repeatable. Of the Silmarils, Fëanor says, " 'Never again shall I make their like' " (*TS*, p. 78). Similarly, Míriel declares of Fëanor, " 'Never again shall I bear child; for strength that would have nourished the life of many has gone forth into Fëanor' " (*TS*, p. 63). Like the Silmarils, Fëanor burns with an inner fire. The crystal of the Silmarils is "but as is the body to the Children of Ilúvatar: the house of its inner fire, that is within it and yet in all parts of it, and is its life" (*TS*, p. 67); Fëanor grows "as if a secret fire were kindled within him" (*TS*, p. 64).

The characteristics of both are deliberately similar. The light of the Silmarils illumines darkness, however black or evil it may be. Because the light is hallowed, those who desire it wrongfully are scorched and burned by it. Fëanor's fire can also illumine—indeed, it is that fire, that light, which enables him alone of all his race to conceive of and to make the Silmarils. But that same fire can and does burn and consume. Like the light of the Silmarils, but even more like the light of the Lamps, Fëanor's inner fire is of such fierceness and intensity that when not properly contained and used it scorches and destroys what it touches. The intensity of his nature drives him both to make and to break, and again we see in him humanity's potential poised on the edge, balanced between light and darkness.

Fëanor is the last and in many ways the most important of the sub-creators who figure in Tolkien's history of the light. His creation is at once a synthesis and a splintering, and thus vividly illustrates the idea of paradox, which runs like a dark thread through the entire mythology. The Silmarils have as their inner fire "the blended light of the Trees of Valinor" (*TS*, p. 67); in them Fëanor has re-combined and made whole the refracted gold and silver light of the Trees. Yet in taking part of that light and enclosing it in jewels he has undeniably fragmented it and created the possibility for further splintering. For the jewels are three discrete units, each of which exists independently of the others. Each can be—and eventually will be—separated from the others. Yet when the Trees are destroyed, the last of the light lives only in the Silmarils and without them would have disappeared entirely from the world. Synthesis in fragmentation and salvation through breaking and dispersal—these are the antinomies of Tolkien's philosophy and the paradoxes of his world.

As for Fëanor himself, his greatest act of creation is also the beginning of his fall. It is clearly meant to recall, but not to recapitulate the Fall of Man. Since a tendency toward evil is inherent in Tolkien's world through the Music, a series of falls replaces the one great Fall of the Judeo-Christian myth. Each is in some manner a fall into self-will and selfishness: Melkor falls prey to the desire to make his own Music instead of subsuming his creative powers to Eru's theme; Fëanor falls prey to the temptation to love and possess his own creations—the Silmarils—and leads his kindred into the Fall of the Noldor. Other falls will come, for in Tolkien's view, "There cannot be any 'story' without a fall—all stories are ultimately about the fall—at least not for human minds as we know them and have them" (*TLOT*, p. 147).

Desire to possess is the cardinal temptation, and possessiveness the great transgression in Tolkien's cosmology, whose only commandment (stated once, but always implicit) is " 'Love not too well the work of thy hands and the devices of thy heart' " (*TS*, p. 125). The fall of the elves, he states unequivocally, "is into possessiveness" (*TLOT*, p. 148).

Tolkien's purpose in introducing the Silmarils into his history becomes clear when he records within two lines the disturbingly similar responses of Fëanor and Melkor to the jewels. We are told that "the heart of Fëanor was fast bound to these things that he himself had made," and in the next sentence we learn that "Melkor lusted for the Silmarils, and the very memory of their radiance was a gnawing fire in his heart" (*TS*, p. 67). Desire to possess the light is superseding desire to live in it. The noontide is declining toward night.

With fitting irony it is Melkor and Fëanor, each once the best and brightest of his kind, who usher in the darkness. Melkor's desire for the Silmarils leads him to sow dissension and mistrust among the Noldor, and to divide them from the Valar. In particular, he works to alienate Fëanor from his half-brothers Fingolfin and Finarfin. The same possessiveness which governs his feeling for the Silmarils leads Fëanor to become jealous of his half-brothers and fear that they may usurp his place. His pride keeps him aloof, and more and more he identifies himself with the Silmarils, wearing them on his brow at feasts. "For Fëanor began to love the Silmarils with a greedy love, and grudged the sight of them to all save to his father and his seven sons; he seldom remembered now that the light within them was not his own" (*TS*, p. 69). For the rest of the time Fëanor withholds the sight of the Silmarils from Valinor, keeping them "locked in the deep chambers of his hoard" (*TS*, p. 69).

Tolkien's use of *hoard* suggests lust for possession, and to anyone familiar with the stories of northern mythology it will inevitably recall the dragon's hoard which in the tales of Sigurd and Beowulf, the two greatest northern heroes, leads only to destruction and death. Here Tolkien is expanding an idea which he explored in a somewhat different context in *The Hobbit,* where the fall of Thorin Oakenshield is the direct result of Thorin's greed for the dragon hoard, and in particular for the Arkenstone, a Silmaril-like gem. The idea was clearly one that occupied Tolkien, for it is of course the thematic cornerstone of *The Lord of the Rings,* wherein lust for the Ring, "the precious," leads to the downfall of those who possess it, and very nearly destroys Frodo before it is itself destroyed.

Tolkien dramatized this concept in three major pieces of fiction, but clearly felt a necessity to develop it theoretically as well, for he again alludes to it in the "Recovery" section of the fairy-story essay. There he writes of the "appropriation" (literally "making one's own") of "things which once attracted us by their glitter, or their colour, or their shape, and we laid hands on them, and locked them in our hoard, acquired them, and acquiring ceased to look at them" (OFS, p. 77). No great leap of imagination is required to apply this to Fëanor, or to find Tolkien's use and re-use of this motif as evidence of his deep philosophical and religious pre-occupation with the human tendency to grasp and to keep, a tendency which turns mankind inward and downward, away from the light. We cannot fail to see Fëanor's appropriation and hoarding of the Silmarils as a perversion of love for the light, and as a ruinous misuse of its essential quality. Light is not to be held, nor worn as personal ornament, nor locked away from sight. Light is not to be the property of anyone, and he who thinks the light is exclusively his has lost sight of it altogether. And in a very real sense Fëanor has lost his ability to see the light. All of his subsequent actions work against him and send him down, down into a darkness at once real, psychological, and spiritual.

If there is one moment in Tolkien's carefully orchestrated sequence of events which can be called the turning point, the hinge of the ensuing action, it is surely Fëanor's moment of decision following the destruction of the Trees. This is the test of his willingness to let go, to give up, a test as momentous as Frodo's at the Cracks of Doom. Like Frodo, Fëanor fails, but unlike Frodo's failure, his failure has no Gollum to reverse it and inadvertently put things right. The scene as Tolkien draws it is an archetypal meeting—almost a clash—between light and dark, and, as always, it is operational on the literal, the psychological, and the symbolic level.

The moment comes at the harvest festival in Valinor, when what has been sown is reaped. The harvest gathers in not only the fruits of the earth but the lies of Melkor and the pride and greed of Fëanor. Fëanor, banished from Aman because of his hostility toward his half-brothers, is summoned to the feast, and agrees to a reconciliation. But neither his presence nor his reconciliation is wholehearted. He refused to wear the Silmarils, leaving them locked in his hoard, and thus denies sight of them to everyone. And to Fingolfin's declaration of forgiveness Fëanor makes no reply, and to his pledge of loyalty answers only, " 'So be it' " (TS, p. 75). His reservation, holding back a part of himself, foreshadows the later withholding which sets the seal upon his doom.

The moment of reconciliation comes at the hour of the mingling of the gold and silver lights, and must be seen as a time of transition. For it is this time that is chosen by Melkor and his dreadful accomplice Ungoliant (surely one of Tolkien's most terrible creations) to invade the feast and attack the Trees. Tolkien's introduction of Ungoliant at this point and for this purpose is further evidence of his pervasive concern with the theme of light perverted. Ungoliant is a huge spider, a beast-shape fearsome and repugnant in itself. With daring invention, Tolkien juxtaposes this spider-shape, normally associated with darkness and shadowed places, with the light. Ungoliant needs light; she craves it more fiercely than Melkor or Fëanor or any other creature in Tolkien's world, for it is her food. She feeds on light, quite literally swallowing it and vomiting it forth as darkness. This must be seen as the most terrible perversion of all, for light meant to shine is thus devoured, turned in on itself, and made into its opposite.

Melkor stabs the Trees, Ungoliant sucks out their light, and the darkness falls. But the Darkness, the Unlight of Ungoliant, is not just darkness in place of light but darkness made out of light—a palpable emptiness which defeats the eye and robs the world of appearance. "The Light failed, but the Darkness that followed was more than loss of light. In that hour was made a Darkness that seemed not lack but a thing with being of its own: for it was indeed made by malice out of Light" (*TS*, p. 76). The darkness that descends on Valinor is itself a paradox; it is the felt presence of an absence—the absence of that light which has been the life of the Blessed Realm.

Note the distinction that Tolkien makes between darkness before light and darkness after light—specifically, darkness where light should be. There are clearly kinds of dark. The darkness of creation before the light of the Lamps is not to be seen as a negative. The elves awake in the starlit darkness of Middle-earth, a darkness characterized by Tom Bombadil in *The Lord of the Rings*, who tells Frodo that he " 'knew the dark under the stars when it was fearless—before the Dark Lord came from Outside' " (*LOTR*, I, p. 182).

Thus, when Fëanor denies Yavanna when she asks him to give back the light of the Silmarils to revive the Trees, he commits a profound error, for he has known the light but will not give it up to dispel the darkness. The moment, presaged in his refusal to let the elves and the Valar see the Silmarils, and in his reserve at the reconciliation with Fingolfin, comes in the night that follows the death of the Trees. His first denial is silence only. When he is urged to speak, Aulë intervenes, the only one to comprehend his torment: " 'Be not hasty! We ask a greater thing than thou knowest. Let him have peace yet awhile' " (*TS*, p. 78). As cherisher of the Noldor, Aulë understands Fëanor's distress. Only Aulë, who freely offered up his creation, can know how hard it is for his fellow maker, and the speech tells us more about him than it does about Fëanor. Tolkien's point is clear: giving up is not easy; it is only right. But Fëanor's decision is to withhold the Silmarils. His statement—" 'This thing I will not do of free will' " (*TS*, p. 79)—recalls Frodo at the Cracks of Doom: " 'I will not do this deed' " (*LOTR*, III, p. 223). And so he sets his seal upon darkness.

A terrible irony is at work here, for the Silmarils are no longer Fëanor's to keep or to let go: while he deliberated with the Valar, Melkor broke into his stronghold and stole the Silmarils. Tolkien's purpose in constructing such irony is complex. First of all, he wants to show that the light so possessively hoarded by Fëanor was not his to give, as it never is. But more important, the incident shows that greed fosters greed, and possessiveness engenders covetousness. Had Fëanor worn the Silmarils to the feast, instead of willfully denying the sight of them to everyone, they would perhaps not have been stolen as they were.

But beyond that—and this is for Tolkien most important—Fëanor's decision in itself, irrespective of his power to make it good, has a profound effect on him. "The Silmarils had passed away," we are told, "and all one it may seem whether Fëanor had said yea or nay to Yavanna; yet had he said yea at the first, before the tidings came from Formenos, it may be that his after deeds would have been other than they were" (*TS*, p. 79). What are we to make of this statement in the context of the Music of creation, which is "as Fate" to all things except men in Tolkien's world? If Fëanor cannot change the Music, how could he make his subsequent deeds "other than they were"? This question is of central importance to an understanding of the working of fate and free will in the mythology. For Fëanor embodies the polarities of light and dark, and in his character the interdependence of those other polarities, fate and free will, is illustrated most clearly. In making the provocative and puzzling statement about Fëanor's choice in saying yea or nay, Tolkien's emphasis is not on the fate of the light nor on the fate, the ultimate destiny, of Fëanor, but rather on his attitude and his motives. If he could have freely given the Silmarils, he would himself have been free of his bondage to them, and his inner darkness might have been lightened. Subsequent *events* would perhaps not be externally different, but Fëanor's motives in them could be different, as could his attitudes toward himself, the Silmarils, and the peoples of his world.

The words of his answer to Yavanna—" 'This thing I will not do of free will. But if the Valar will constrain me . . .' " (*TS*, p. 79)—reveal his limited perception of himself and the forces in his world. His view of freedom is limited to the immediate context; he is conscious only of his will pitted against that of the Valar. Within the context of the Music, Fëanor's answer would seem to be meaningless. He cannot alter fate, and the fate of the Silmarils is out of his hands. What he describes as the constraint of the Valar is also meaningless, because they cannot constrain him any more than they can constrain Melkor—they can only request that he comply with their wishes. For Fëanor to accede to their request would be for him to acknowledge a higher necessity than his own, and this he cannot do. Here Tolkien has deliberately constructed a situation in which Fëanor's decision can affect nothing and no one but himself to show that in the fictive world of The Silmarillion free will is more important as a matter of internal governance than as a determiner of external events. The Music always has the same form, but how it is played (to extend the metaphor), whether fast or slow, *allegro* or *andante,* is up to the performers.

Fëanor is not free, not because he is bound by the Music but because he is in bondage to his own creation. His determination to cling to that bondage in a situation where he could give it up determines the subsequent direction of his character as well as the character of all the events which lead out from it. It leads him to his oath of vengeance which haunts his sons throughout their lives in Middle-earth and binds them to a vendetta which they cannot abandon, however much they come to hate it. It leads to the exodus of the Noldor from Aman in their desire to dominate Middle-earth, to rule kingdoms at their own will, and to be "lords of the unsullied Light" (*TS,* p. 83). And it leads to the theft of the White Ships and the great sin of the Kinslaying, a deed whose repercussions reach far beyond the doers to affect the lives of those yet unborn. The death of Finrod, the character of Maeglin, and the fall of Gondolin are all events directly traceable to the Kinslaying.

The Kinslaying and the theft of the White Ships from the Teleri, two deeds which occur as part of the same event, show the reader how far Fëanor has fallen. At the same time they are acts which push him even farther into the abyss. For in taking the White Ships to fulfill his own need, unheeding of the protests and the needs of the Teleri, he is re-enacting Melkor's theft of the Silmarils. The White Ships are the proudest handiwork of the Teleri, creations which are to them—as they tell Fëanor—" 'as are the gems of the Noldor: the work of our hearts, whose like we shall not make again' " (*TS,* p. 86). The comparison with the Silmarils is explicit— and just as explicit is the contrast between their refusal to yield their ships to Fëanor and his refusal to yield the Silmarils to Yavanna. But they are right to refuse his request, which is negative and destructive both in desire and in execution. Fëanor, on the other hand, was wrong to refuse Yavanna's request, which was positive and would have benefited all the world.

Moreover, Fëanor is lacking in that very understanding

which the loss of the Silmarils should have given him: how it feels to be deprived of one's most precious work. The contrast here is with Aulë, who, because he could give up his own creation, knew Fëanor's anguish and understood his hesitation. Because he could not relinquish his creation, Fëanor has killed his capacity to understand or care about the Teleri. His determination to have the ships by any means leads to the Kinslaying, and even those innocent of his intent, such as Fingon and Fingolfin, are caught in his guilt and will be haunted by it to their deaths. This first killing of elf by elf is analogous to the murder of Abel by Cain, and the Noldor are doomed as Cain was. The words of Mandos, " 'Ye have spilled the blood of your kindred unrighteously and have stained the land of Aman' " (TS, p. 88), make clear the enormity of the sin and of Fëanor's fall.

For "the marring of Fëanor," as Tolkien makes clear, is no less evil a deed than the killing of the Trees: it is "of the works of Melkor one of the most evil" (TS, p. 98). As Fëanor was the greatest of the Noldor, the brightest and the best and by far the most creative, so he becomes the darkest and the most destructive. "The best corrupted is the worst" is a text Tolkien returns to again and again—with Melkor, with Fëanor, with Thingol, with Saruman, with the men of Númenor. " 'Nothing is evil in the beginning' " Elrond says to Frodo. " 'Even Sauron was not so' " (LOTR, I, p. 351). And nowhere does he better illustrate the maxim than in the drama of the fall of Fëanor. Fëanor's greatest virtues are his greatest flaws, his darkness simply the obverse of his brightness. At every step his desires control him, yet he cannot perceive this flaw. He is most bound when he thinks himself most free, most ripe for evil when he thinks he is escaping it. In short, paradox defines Fëanor: light leads him into darkness; the light of the Silmarils blinds him to himself; his most creative act leads him into destruction; his making is breaking. And the ultimate inversion of good, his refusal to un-make the Silmarils in order to re-make the Trees, leads him and his people to disastrous fragmentation. He breaks the Noldor away from Aman and from their Eldarin kindred. He breaks faith with the Teleri at Alqualondë. And he breaks with his own family in abandoning Fingolfin at Araman. Fëanor's obsession with the light, his need to possess it, divides families, sows mistrust and hatred, and engenders feud and revenge. When they return to Middle-earth the Noldor are a divided people, marred by an internal strife which breeds more strife and echoes down the ages.

Fëanor's own destruction swiftly follows the death of the Trees and the pall of darkness which covers the Blessed Realm. In his fruitless war with Morgoth he is "consumed by the flame of his own wrath," and in his furious rage he overreaches himself, pursuing his enemy "far ahead of the van of his own host" (*TS*, p. 107). Surrounded by the forces of Morgoth, he is "wrapped in fire and wounded with many wounds" (*TS*, p. 107). Thus Fëanor, Spirit of Fire, is himself destroyed by fire. Wrapped in fire and consumed by his own flame, he burns out and is burnt out, for "so fiery was his spirit that as it sped his body fell to ash, and was borne away like smoke; and his likeness has never again appeared in Arda, neither has his spirit left the halls of Mandos" (*TS*, p. 107). Like the Trees, like the Silmarils, like the White Ships, Fëanor was unique, a creation never to be repeated.

But his legacy, both for good and for ill, lives on in the world he has helped to change. The Silmarils, the last splinters of the light, keep that light alive as a hope and a vision. Fëanor's sons continue his pursuit; the sins of the father are visited upon the children in their obligation to uphold his Oath. Though they come to hate the burden of that Oath, they are afraid to let it go, and thus are prisoners of his will. And, for good and ill, the Noldor have returned to Middle-earth, bringing with them all the gifts which make them great and all the flaws which make them vulnerable, infusing the life of Middle-earth with all their skill and their art, all their capacity to create and to divide.

For the process must go on. Light, language, and peoples will continue to impinge upon one another, and the process, as can be expected, will be turbulent. Progressive darkening will be lighted by unexpected courage, great beauty, enduring loyalty. Light and dark will come together again and again, both literally and metaphorically, as the Music plays itself out.

VI
LIGHT OUT OF DARKNESS

Through darkness one may come to the light.

TOLKIEN, UNFINISHED TALES

In the events following the darkening of the Trees, splintered light, contained in the Silmarils and in the Noldor who pursue them, returns to Middle-earth. And now the fragmentation and diminution of both light and peoples accelerates. It is as if the downhill spiral into spiritual and psychological darkness has suddenly steepened, with a concomitant increase in momentum and inability to slow down. The gathering darkness is broken from time to time by flashes of light, some vivid, some dim, all seeming brighter for their contrast with the surrounding dark. Light and dark are the established polarities of existence, each deriving meaning from the other, each giving meaning to the struggle which is human life. That struggle becomes the focus of the story. The action centers in the elven kingdoms of Middle-earth, both those of the Sindar and those realms newly established by the returning Noldor.

And now individual personality, the variousness of human nature, first introduced with Fëanor, begins actively determining the direction of events. We are shown a spectrum of personalities of varying shades of light and dark: Thingol, Maeglin, Turgon, Eöl, Idril, Lúthien. All of these, through actions and reactions arising out of their natures, move the world and shape its future. But these elves, Noldoran and Sindarin, are no longer alone in their world. They are joined by Húrin, Tuor, Beren, Túrin—a catalogue of heroic newcomers. For co-incident with the return of the Noldor and the Silmarils to Middle-earth, Tolkien brings into his history the Followers, the Younger Children of Ilúvatar—mortal men.

In philosophical terms, this would seem at first to be an unnecessary complication. All worlds are complex, even those deceptively simple mythic ones whose stories explore the relationship between man and God. Tolkien's world is already equipped to deal with that through the elves. But he has chosen to introduce another distinct, sentient species, and the rest of the narrative deals with the interaction of men and elves with one another and with the world around them. With the introduction of men, Tolkien is tied a little closer to observed reality, for they must be men as we know them if we are to recognize and empathize with them. Elves, however human in their psychology, are the stuff of fantasy. Their invention frees Tolkien to use them as he will, and to contrast them with men. The presence of both allows Tolkien to explore certain contrasts, contrasts which are sharper for being embodied in two races. Deathlessness and death, memory and desire, the need for the world and the need to leave it can be seen more clearly when they are imaged in separate peoples.

The initial separation, the turn away from light toward dark, has been developed through the elves. Though it is literally dark when they leave Valinor, they leave the light nonetheless, for Valinor is still the Blessed Realm; it is metaphorically and symbolically light. In contrast, Middle-earth is dark, both literally and metaphorically, lighted only by stars. It has the presence of Melian and Thingol—both of the light—and their people, the Grey-elves. But it is dominated by the unseen presence of Melkor, now called Morgoth, the Black Enemy, the Dark Lord who has hidden in his stronghold the last light of the Silmarils.

Unlike the elves, men have never known the light, never seen it. No one summoned them to Valinor. They come to consciousness, as did the elves, in Middle-earth. But where elves were called into the light, men awake after that light has died. The Trees are a legend, the Silmarils a rumor, a hidden treasure heard of but never seen. Men thus have no direct experience of the light of Aman. They awake with the first rising of the sun, and the only light they see is the earthly daily light of the sun, the inconstant light of the moon, and the flickering of the stars. Sun and moon are themselves remnants, the last fruit and the last flower of the Trees, reminders of the light that is gone. They are light enough to live by and to work by, but they are a long way from the unearthly light that made Valinor the Blessed Realm. Their light is interrupted by periods of real dark, with only stars to break it. Thus Tolkien has brought light to its lowest ebb without making it go out altogether, for he clearly means sun and moon to be light that is qualitatively different from the light of the Trees. "The Light of Sun (or Moon)," he says, "is derived from the Trees only after they were sullied by Evil" (*TLOT*, p. 148). Yet it is worth noting that the sun and moon are fruit and flower, suggesting a ripening, unfolding process in the nature of men whose only outer light they are.

At the metaphorical level, darkness and light acquire directional character in Tolkien's world, beginning with the source of light in Valinor and developing as Morgoth flees eastward into darkness, followed by the Noldor. Two great tides of movement surge across the landscape. They are, in broadest terms, the movement of elves from west to east, and the corresponding movement of men from east to west. These are not just migrations but responses to light and darkness, both literal and metaphorical. And they establish a pattern which illustrates in concrete terms one of the central concerns of the entire work—how best to seek and find the light, and how best to benefit from it. This pattern is not a smooth one, for Tolkien does not write in terms of simple movements west to east and east to west. There are contrary impulses in both sweeps, eddies and swirls in which the movement swerves, checks itself, or turns back on itself. Nevertheless, the general pattern is constant and, as always with Tolkien, works at once literally, metaphorically, and symbolically.

At the literal level it has to do with sun and moon. After some initial adjustments, these bodies assume the courses of sun and moon in our own world; that is, they rise in the east, cross the heavens, and set in the west. Thus, in going toward the east of their world, the elves are going against the light, a movement which almost immediately assumes metaphorical dimension. What Tolkien is using here is commonly called the widdershins impulse, which in folk belief is traditionally negative, bringing bad luck. The dictionary defines *widder-shins* or *withershins* as "in the opposite direction; in reverse; counterclockwise." To go "widdershins" is to go "in a direction opposite to the course of the sun." The word itself comes from Old High German *widar*, "against," plus *sinnes*, the genitive of *sin*, "journey." It is thus the direction of "the journey against," the journey in opposition to the light. The Indo-European bases of *widdershins* are *wi-*, "apart, in half," and *sent-*, "to head for, go." In its earliest formulation, then, the word contains some concept of division and the impulse toward separation. This is entirely in harmony with Tolkien's history, for the development of the elves, both cultural and linguistic, has been in the direction of division, fragmentation, and separation from the light. Their impulse to go against the light will contrast with the instinctive impulse of men to go toward the light, even though they have never seen it.

This elven impulse away from light is manifest not only in the eastward journey of the Noldor but within them as individuals, in their interactions and interminglings. This impulse is illustrated at its most negative in the character and actions of the half-Noldor/half-Sindar Maeglin. By his parentage Maeglin is a mixture, a combination of light, half-light, and dark in whom dark predominates. As such, he is a model of what may happen when light goes toward its opposite. Maeglin is the son of an ill-matched couple who themselves exhibit inexplicable impulses toward the dark. His mother is Aredhel Ar-Feiniel, called the White Lady of the Noldor. Against her nature she marries Eöl, a kinsman of Thingol's people, and thus a Grey-elf. But he is called the Dark Elf, both because of his nature and because of his tendency to seek the dark and dwell in it. He lives far to the east in Middle-earth, in the forest of Nan Elmoth. Thus Maeglin is born and grows up in shadow, and when he goes toward the light he brings that shadow with him. He is named Maeglin, "Sharp Glance," but his mother's nickname for him is Lómion, "Child of the Twilight." It is a fitting epithet, for as Maeglin grows he physically resembles the Noldor, his mother's people, "but in mood and mind he was the son of his father" (*TS*, p. 134). Externally light, he is internally dark, a light declining toward night.

His function in the story is that of hidden darkness within light, a darkness which eventually overcomes that light, at least in part. Returning westward with his mother to her home in the hidden kingdom of Gondolin, Maeglin is welcomed by her brother, Turgon, king of Gondolin. Though he stands high in Turgon's favor, his love for Turgon's daughter Idril (Sparkling Brilliance), while it is an attraction of dark toward light, is perverse and twisted, for Idril, his first cousin, is too close by kinship to marry him. Furthermore, she does not love him, and is made uneasy by his love for her. Maeglin ultimately betrays Gondolin to Morgoth after being captured and tortured. As inner darkness, he brings about the downfall of one of the most powerful and beautiful of the elven strongholds of Middle-earth. As the Child of Twilight he has brought darkness with him out of the east.

This is the most negative, least hopeful outcome of the elven impulse toward the east. In a different mode, an eastern journey of Finrod Felagund, an elven prince, works indirectly toward the light. Finrod is the eldest son of one of Fëanor's half-brothers, Finarfin, whose mother was a Vanyar, a Fair Elf. Because of his nature he is one of the best and the brightest of the Noldor in Middle-earth. And Finrod is the first of the Noldor to encounter the Second Children of Ilúvatar, a meeting that could stand as a paradigmatic encounter between elves and men. Hunting "east of [the river] Sirion," Finrod wearies of the chase, and continuing far into the east, he comes across a strange people wandering westward over the mountains. When he questions them about their origins, the men can tell Finrod very little, for they, unlike elves, have almost no memory of their beginnings and their early history. " 'A darkness lies behind us,' " says Bëor, their leader, " 'and we have turned our backs upon it, and we do not desire to return thither even in thought. Westwards our hearts have been turned, and we believe that there we shall find Light' " (*TS*, p. 141).

Men are seeking the light. Without having known it, without any sure way to reach it, they are drawn to it, and are in the process of taking themselves out of the dark. A statement such as Bëor's makes clear the contrast between men and elves, and the function of each in Tolkien's world. But their function goes beyond providing contrast for one another. For the two kinds do not simply inhabit the same space—they work with (and sometimes against) one another. They interact, ultimately intermarry, and cross each other's paths and destinies again and again; they seem to need one another. They are both Children of Ilúvatar, deriving directly from the Godhead, both instrumental in working out his purpose.

The key is in the underlying nature of the directional movement, and can be most clearly seen at the points of intersection, where the path of westward-moving, light-seeking man crosses that of eastward-moving, light-shunning elf. The primary encounter is that between Finrod and Bëor, the outcome of which is important. Finrod befriends the men he meets, singing to them of the making of the world and the bliss of Valinor, that light which they are seeking; he puts their existence in a context. Beyond that, he acts as a guide, for Bëor and his people ally themselves with Finrod and follow him westward as he returns from his hunting journey. He directs them along the right path and reinforces their westward impulse.

Another such encounter between man and elf occurs at the beginning of the first of Tolkien's *Unfinished Tales*, that "Of Tuor and his Coming to Gondolin." In the turmoil of the constant wars with Morgoth which rack Middle-earth, Tuor, a man, sets out in search of Turgon and the Hidden Kingdom of Gondolin. The purpose behind Tuor's journey, a purpose of the Valar and in particular of Ulmo, Lord of the Waters, is to bring about his union with Turgon's daughter Idril—the first union of men and elves. Tuor himself is not aware of this purpose, but seems to be following blind impulse.

Tuor travels westward, led by an impulse he does not understand toward a destination not yet revealed to him. On the third day of his journey he is unexpectedly checked. The stream which he has been following as an omen since it sprang up at his feet flows under a seemingly impassable rock wall. As darkness falls, Tuor halts, bitter and thwarted by what appears to be the failure of his omen. At dawn of the next day he sees two elves, Gelmir and Arminas, following the stream east through a passage from the far side of the rock wall. Tuor tells them of his journey and his frustration with the stream which has "gone into darkness." In reply, Gelmir voices Tolkien's (and perhaps Eru's) theme: " 'Through darkness one may come to the light.' "[1] This is a literal re-alization of the metaphoric and symbolic pattern underlying the interaction of light and dark in Tolkien's world. With the primary light no longer present, the only way to the light is through darkness—a darkness at once physical, mental, and spiritual.

Gelmir's next words to Tuor reinforce this realization and suggest at least part of Tolkien's purpose in creating two races: " 'Through darkness you shall come to the light. We will set your feet on the road, but we cannot guide you far. . . .' "[2] The change in verb from *may* to *shall* is notable and important. As a lover of old meaning, Tolkien was perfectly aware of the difference between the Old English verbs *ma-gan* (may) and *sculan* (shall). The first denotes ability, while the second, unlike its modern English equivalent, denotes external necessity, that which must happen, that which is fated. By whatever means he can, using whatever help he comes across, man is going to find the light.

This encounter between man and elf, and the elf's words, are as explicit a statement as can be found of Tolkien's in-tended use of the two races. Elf moving away from the light meets man making his way toward it. Paths cross, with be-neficent results for man. The elves know where they are going; man has only an impulse and a wayward sign to guide him. His passage toward the light will take him through dark-ness. Elves, going in the opposite direction, can set him on the right path, but they cannot guide him far. Why this should be so, why elves can point out the path but cannot guide man

[1] J. R. R. Tolkien, *Unfinished Tales of Númenor and Middle-earth*, ed. Christopher Tolkien (Boston: Houghton Mifflin, 1980), p. 21.

[2] Tolkien, *Unfinished Tales*, p. 21.

along it, comes to the heart of Tolkien's vision. The way to the light must be followed independently, with no steady guide but the inner impulse.

By separating the impulse to seek the light from the impulse to turn away from it (both typical of mankind in the real world), Tolkien is able to use elves and men to place each impulse in sharp focus and to develop the possibilities inherent in each. For each is a powerful force, and both are simultaneously at work in his world, as they are in ours. Moreover, by physically crossing the paths of men and elves, Tolkien is able to develop as fully as possible the necessary interaction of dark and light as elements of the pattern potentiated in the Music.

The pattern here described of west and east, light and dark, men and elves is material evidence of the opposition, the conflict, set up in the Music, and does much to clarify the role of Melkor/Morgoth in the creation and continuing affairs of the world. Elves and men are a separate part of creation. As Children of Ilúvatar they are described as coming directly from the Godhead into the world. There is no intermediary agency; the Ainur have no part in their creation, and therefore do not fully understand them. Yet for all their directness of origin, elves and men find their lives complicated and profoundly affected by all that came before them, most especially the primal rebellion of Melkor.

In those early moments of creation and rebellion, Eru propounds three successive themes. The first and second themes are interrupted by Melkor, who introduces his own themes, producing discord in the Music. Eru's third theme, begun in response to Melkor's disruption of the other two, takes Melkor's continuing discord and his continuing efforts to drown out Eru's Music with his own theme, and weaves it into the Music.

> For it seemed at first soft and sweet, a mere rippling of gentle sounds in delicate melodies; but it could not be quenched, and it took to itself power and profundity. And it seemed at last that there were two musics progressing at one time before the seat of Ilúvatar, and they were utterly at variance. The one was deep and

wide and beautiful, but slow and blended with an immeasurable sorrow, from which its beauty chiefly came.
The other had now achieved a unity of its own; but it
was loud, and vain, and endlessly repeated; and it had
little harmony, but rather a clamorous unison as of
many trumpets braying upon a few notes. And it es-
sayed to drown the other music by the violence of its
voice, but it seemed that its most triumphant notes
were taken by the other and woven into its own solemn
pattern. (TS, pp. 16-17)

It is this third theme which brings with it the Children
of Ilúvatar, this theme which is "blended with an immeasurable sorrow" and which is the direct result of Melkor's
rebellion. After Melkor—and this perhaps to some degree
because of him—come elves and men. Their lives are to be
lived in a world of immeasurable sorrow, but as part of a
pattern which can take the most triumphant notes of the
discord and weave them in.

Elves are bound by the patterns of the Music, not necessarily within themselves but in the external events of their
lives. Men are not. They are given by Ilúvatar "a virtue to
shape their life . . . beyond the Music of the Ainur, which is
as fate to all things else; and of their operation everything
should be, in form and deed, completed, and the world fulfilled unto the last and smallest" (TS, pp. 41-42). The interaction of men and elves, then, is the interplay of free will and
destiny within the design. Tolkien clearly intends both to be
powerful forces in his world, and perhaps envisions each as
a necessary function of the other. For there can be no freedom
in willing unless there is something to be free from. The
destinies of elves will inevitably affect the free choices of
men, and the choices of men will have the power to alter the
destinies of elves.

Tolkien is not drawing a simple pattern of two contrast-
ing paths intersecting. His world, like ours, is more complex
and more interesting than that; it is much more a tapestry
than a map. There are elves such as the Vanyar who find the
light and never leave it. There are elves such as Finrod who
turn unwillingly from the light but carry some glimmer of it

always with them. And there are elves such as Fëanor and Thingol, who turn unknowingly toward the dark, never aware of when or how they have gone wrong. Men, too, are shown in varying shades of dark and light. Tuor goes through darkness into light. Beren goes from light into dark and back out into light again, or, as Sam Gamgee describes it to Frodo, " 'past happiness and into grief and beyond it' " (*LOTR*, II, p. 321). Húrin cries out, " '*Aurë entuluva*! Day shall come again!' " as he fights a losing battle against the forces of Morgoth (*TS*, p. 195). The life of his son, Túrin, is a furious headlong rush into darkness, hastened by every effort he makes to find the light.

This may be philosophy, but it is philosophy couched as fiction, and Tolkien does not explain his tapestry, he displays it. Nowhere does he more vividly present his theme than in the pictured interaction of Thingol, Lúthien, and Beren—elven king, elven princess, and mortal man. Lúthien is the daughter of Thingol and Melian, and in her person is one of those manifestations of light that from time to time illumine the darkness of Middle-earth. Her light is indwelling and inherent, since she is the child of Melian, who has lived in the light of the Trees, and of Thingol, who has seen the light even though he turned away from it. If there were an aristocracy of light in Middle-earth (and Tolkien hints at it, though he is not explicit), Lúthien would certainly be its crown princess, for she is of the "strain of the Ainur who were with Ilúvatar before Eä" (*TS*, p. 56).

Lúthien is light, albeit light dimmed and diminished, as far removed from its source in the light of the Trees as she is physically removed from Aman. And Tolkien's words to describe her evoke images of diminished light. Her eyes are "grey as the starlit evening"; her hair is "dark as the shadows of twilight"; her beauty is "as the light upon the leaves of trees . . . as the stars above the mists of the world" (*TS*, p. 165). Beren sees her first "at a time of evening under moonrise," and again at "a time near dawn on the eve of spring" (*TS*, p. 165). All is dimmed, shadowed, reflected, or misted over. The very times when Beren sees her are times of changing and diminished light.

As might be expected, this idea of diminished light shows up in the language as the reflection and expression of perception. When Beren first sees Lúthien, he does not know her name or who she is. Since she is singing, he calls her Tinúviel, a Sindarin word meaning "daughter of twilight" and a poetic name for the nightingale. It inevitably recalls Maeglin's epithet, Child of the Twilight, and the similarity is no coincidence. Both names suggest aspects of diminished light. But whereas Maeglin is the offspring of light seeking darkness and going further and further into the dark, Lúthien is the last glimmer of the true light, in human form what the Silmarils are as jewels—embodiment of all the remaining light.

Like Melian, and Yavanna whom Melian served, Lúthien is a singer. Her namesake, the nightingale, is a singer of twilight, of lessened light. In Beren's name for her, light and sound are once more joined, but with an unmistakable diminution descending from the choirs of the Ainur, through the song by which Yavanna made the Trees down to the twilight song of Lúthien Tinúviel.

The etymology of Tinúviel is worth examining. It comes from the compounding of two Primitive Eldarin word-elements, *tin-*, "sparkle," and *dōmē*, "dusk." From *dōmē* comes Quenya *lómë* and Sindarin *dú*, "dimness, dusk." Combined with *lin-*, a root meaning "sing, make a musical sound," *lómë* and *dú* form Quenya *lómelindë* and Sindarin *dúlin*, literally "dusk-song" or "dusk-singer." Both mean "nightingale." The compound *tin-dómē*, "starry twilight," from which come Quenya *tindómerel* and Sindarin *tinúviel*, poetically links song and starry twilight as a name for the nightingale. As an epithet for Lúthien it is fitting, for she is not only the literal daughter of diminished light but a singer whose song is instrumental in the recovery of a Silmaril, that last splinter of the light from the Trees.

Like her mother, Melian, Lúthien has a shining light in her face, but we are not told, as we were with Melian, that it is the light of Ilúvatar. The question is left open, for Lúthien is farther from Aman, much more of Middle-earth. But it is Middle-earth that needs the light now, in whatever form it appears. Men must find the light however they can. The meeting of Beren and Lúthien is a deliberate re-staging of the meeting between Thingol and Melian, with one notable difference. Like Thingol, Beren first sees his beloved in the woods, and like Thingol, he falls in love at first sight. But unlike Thingol, who turns back from the light to love Melian, Beren's love leads him toward the light. He has been fleeing from Morgoth, the Dark Lord, and in his encounter with Lúthien he is going toward light, away from dark.

Unlike Melian's light, Lúthien's light is fitful, for she vanishes from Beren's sight, and his pursuit of her is at once a quest for the beloved, in good medieval romance tradition, and an enactment of every mortal man's quest for the light. Without sight of her he is "as one that is stricken with sudden blindness, and seeks with hands to grasp the vanished light" (*TS*, p. 165). What was ordinary vision before he saw her becomes like blindness once he has seen her and then sees her no more.

Both literally and metaphorically, the paths of Beren and Thingol intersect. The meeting point is Lúthien, the treasure that Beren desires and the treasure that Thingol hopes to keep. In his pride and his possessiveness of his daughter, Thingol demands a Silmaril from Morgoth's Iron Crown as her price and Beren's test of worthiness. But it is a greater test than Thingol knows, a test for him as well as for Beren. For while Beren has been struggling toward the light, Thingol, in ways at first almost unnoticeable, has been turning further and further from it.

Only on the thematic level do his actions appear unjustified; on the plot level they are valid and backed by political and dynastic necessity. Thingol's kingdom of Doriath, hidden, like Turgon's Gondolin and Finrod's kindgom of Nargothrond against the invasions of Morgoth, has been an island of peace amid the wars of Middle-earth. His people are Grey-elves, technically Moriquendi but described as the fairest and wisest and most skillful of all the elves of Middle-earth. The word *fair* recalls the epithet of the Vanyar—Fair Elves—and so lifts the Sindar well above the other elves. True of his people, this is even more true of Thingol, described as "great among the Eldar . . . not accounted among the Moriquendi, but with the Elves of the Light, mighty upon Middle-earth" (*TS*, p. 56).

With the return of the Noldor to Middle-earth, however, Thingol's character begins to darken, and, on the plot level, not without reason. The incursion of new peoples into Middle-earth is potentially detrimental to the security of his kingdom and the freedom of his people, and thus he keeps them out. He gives the Noldor permission to dwell in the empty lands outside Doriath, but does not allow them in his kingdom except as invited guests. Thingol's motive for this action fits Tolkien's world view, which sees evil as beginning always with the perception of apparent good or apparent necessity. And it is of a piece with Thingol's character, which has chosen the dimmed light and dimmed perception of Middle-earth over the clear light of Aman. At its core, Thingol's action is possessive, and foreshadows things to come. In political terms his territorial imperative is justifiable, but it anticipates that greater, less reasonable possessiveness which he feels for Lúthien and which he will come to feel for the Silmaril.

His next action is less sound and much darker, both literally and metaphorically. It has to do with language and the interaction of languages and peoples. As the Sindar and the Noldor meet and interact in Middle-earth, the Noldor quickly pick up Sindarin, whereas the Sindar are slow to learn Quenya. (Fuller light and perception can comprehend the lesser, while the lesser cannot encompass the greater.) The inevitable result is that the Noldor begin to speak Sindarin in order to help communication. Thus their very facility betrays them, and they gradually abandon the language of light for the language of twilight. Quenya is kept as a language of lore, but eventually becomes something like Latin in the modern world, known and read but not spoken.

The process is social as well as linguistic: "In many parts of the land the Noldor and the Sindar became welded into one people, and spoke the same tongue" (*TS*, p. 117). The assimilation of the Noldor into the life of Middle-earth occurs largely through language, and works to subtly alter them. Words express perception, but by the same token they can alter it. In abandoning Quenya for Sindarin the Noldor exchange one mode of perception for another; they become more in tune with the character and beauty of Middle-earth. The farther from Aman—the once literal, now metaphoric source of the light—the weaker becomes the light itself, and the perception of it.

Thingol, operating out of his own nature instead of in the light, pushes the abandonment of light still further. After learning of the Kinslaying at Alqualondë in which the Noldor slew many of his own people, the Teleri, he forbids Quenya to be spoken in his realm. " 'Never again in my ears shall be heard the tongue of those who slew my kin in Alqualondë! Nor in all my realm shall it be openly spoken, while my power endures. All the Sindar shall hear my command that they shall neither speak with the tongue of the Noldor nor answer to it' " (*TS*, p. 129). In equating the language with the deeds of its speakers, Thingol is disastrously confusing perceptions. He is unable to separate light from the uses to which it may be wrongly put. In this he is not unlike Fëanor. Indeed, a resemblance between Thingol and Fëanor builds gradually from this point on, for both, in following their own natures, become increasingly blind to the light.

Thingol's prohibition of Quenya is formative, for it affects all of elven Middle-earth, and men as well. What has been *de facto* in practice has now been made *de jure*. Thingol has legislated the language of light out of use, "for the Sindar heard his word, and thereafter throughout Beleriand they refused the tongue of the Noldor, and shunned those that spoke it aloud; but the Exiles took the Sindarin tongue in all their daily uses . . ." (*TS*, p. 129).

In forbidding the use of Quenya, Thingol for all practical purposes is forbidding light, for he is rejecting the opportunity to spiritually enrich the Sindar through the infusion of greater brightness into their language and their perceptions. Further, he is creating a situation which will lead to the further diminution and spiritual impoverishment of the Noldor. And within his own personal destiny he is ranging himself against the light. He originally turned away from the light, but now he is turning the light away from himself. It is a second rejection, a second missed opportunity. Thingol is narrowing his options.

The cumulative effect of his actions—each understandable, even justifiable in itself—is to lead him further and further from the light and from the proper understanding of it, so that when he gains possession of the light in the form of a Silmaril he does not know how to appreciate it nor how best to use it. Both of his negative decisions—forbidding free access to Doriath and prohibiting the speaking of Quenya in his kingdom or by his people—work to further darken a character whose tendency toward the dark is already evident in the making of those decisions. Again, a comparison with Fëanor is apt, for the same self-darkening behavior caught Fëanor in the circular darkness of the Kinslaying and the burning of the ships. The diminution of light suggested by the alteration of his name from Elwë to Elu, from Singollo to Thingol, the whole implication of dimness inherent in the epithet "Greycloak" deepens with each decision he makes. The path, once taken, is difficult to turn back from.

His next step down into the dark is the demand for a Silmaril as the bride-price for Lúthien. This request, which comes from a compound of motives, has complex effects that reach far beyond the initial actions, effects both negative and positive, bringing both darkness and light. It fixes Thingol's own doom and that of his kingdom. Paradoxically, it also restores the light of a Silmaril to a darkened world, and sets the stage for Eärendil's journey to Valinor to plead for both elves and men.

The task Thingol sets Beren—to bring him a Silmaril from Morgoth's Iron Crown—is the traditional, seemingly impossible quest typical of medieval romance. But in the context of Tolkien's world it has a double force, working against Thingol and for Beren. The quest demand will help Thingol save face (for he has sworn not to kill Beren) but will also bring about Beren's death, and thus deny him Lúthien. Thingol has no intention of giving up Lúthien to Beren, but his possessiveness is matched by the acquisitiveness which makes him desire a Silmaril.

On the face of it, what Thingol proposes seems to be a

direct exchange of light for light, the light of Lúthien for the light of a Silmaril. But Tolkien's thesis is that light is not to be possessed. It is, after all, not so much a thing in itself as something to see by. Light at its best is meant to reveal, to make visible, so that we may see clearly and thus judge rightly. We may use it—indeed, we are meant to use it—but we may not hold it. And this applies to light in any form. Thus Thingol's possessiveness of Lúthien is wrongful, just as his desire to possess a Silmaril is wrongful. Moreover, in a psychologically real sense, Lúthien's light is not his to give; it is hers. And she has already given herself to Beren, when "beyond his hope she returned to him where he sat in darkness, and . . . laid her hand in his" (*TS*, p. 166). Light is its own possession, to shine where it must. But Thingol no longer has the capacity to comprehend this; his perceptions and his motives are darkened and twisted. With irony more bitter than he knows, he uses the word *jewel* to refer to both Lúthien and the Silmaril, a descriptive choice that is telling evidence of how far he has fallen away from the light and how obscured his own vision has become. To regard either form of light as ornament or possession is to be blind to its real purpose and real worth. The transaction he proposes to Beren—Lúthien for a Silmaril—is designed to secure light for himself no matter what happens. The pawn of his own desires, he wants the one light yet cannot bring himself to give up the other. The parallel with Fëanor, both in obsessive desire for the light and in lack of self-knowledge, is unmistakable.

Beren's path runs counter to Thingol's, but where they intersect the fates of both are involved. Each is instrumental in the other's destiny, and the actions of both help to determine the future of the Silmaril and of the two races of elves and men. Here again, as with Fëanor, the interaction of fate and free will is crucial. But in this case the situation is more complex than in Tolkien's previous treatment of the motif. For here Tolkien counterpoises the Music against the creator-bestowed power of men to go beyond the Music and to have their choices affect events. Who does what to whom, and how, becomes the question. In terms of the outcome of events, the answer is not easily determined. If Thingol's fate is contained within the Music and Beren has the power to shape his life beyond the Music, how do the two lives affect one another? Is Thingol's fate determined, but triggered by his meeting with Beren? Is Beren's quest for the Silmaril determined by Thingol's decree? By his love for Lúthien? How much has the Music affected their meeting and their love for one another? The train of events set in motion by their meeting includes the death of Finrod, the recovery of the Silmaril, the death of Thingol, the death and transfiguration of Beren and Lúthien, the Voyage of Eärendil, and the defeat of Morgoth.

Whatever the outcome of events, it would seem that in this situation, as in the decision of Fëanor, Tolkien's emphasis is on motive. Free will seems to be most powerful and most perceptible in its inner manifestations rather than in the interaction of externally observable events. Where Thingol is motivated by possessiveness and greed, Beren is motivated by love. Both their courses of action must be judged as much for their reasons as for their effects.

Thingol, ruled by the Music, has no control over events, but he does have the power to respond to them well or ill. His death is determined; but how he dies—for a good purpose or an evil one—is within his power to control. His actions, therefore, must be seen and valued in the context of his motives as well as of their effects. And therein lies the paradox, for his motives are twisted, and the outcome of his actions is both bad and good. Death and destruction follow his obsession with the Silmaril, his own death not the least. Yet through him that Silmaril is recovered, to be a sign of hope to elves and men. Beren and Lúthien come together, and in their child, Dior, they begin the half-elven race which combines all that is best of elves and men.

Beren's motives, which contribute as much to this course of events, are quite different from Thingol's motives. They are straight, not devious, inspired by love rather than greed. And Beren is aided by Lúthien, whose choices as an elf coincide with and even further his choices as a man. Lúthien's part in the interaction of elves and men, of fate and free will, is both active and symbolic. For she embodies, as does the Silmaril, what is left of the light. In loving her, Beren is manifesting what must surely be understood at this point in the history as the right way to seek and find the light—through human love, which at its highest leads to divine love. Where Thingol allowed love for the reflected light in Melian to lead him away from the light of the Trees, in this less visibly holy time Beren finds light in Lúthien which leads him toward the true light. He is not consciously seeking this light, for men have never seen it. Yet he follows the path, an upward path to which, inadvertently echoing the action of Gelmir and Arminas, Thingol has directed him.

Thingol's path, in contrast, continues its downward course, and the angle of decline becomes progressively more precipitous. The steepening is scarcely perceptible at first. Because Thingol has been great, it takes a long time for the light inherent in his name to dim so much that it goes out altogether. Even after the completion of the quest for the Silmaril his greatness counterbalances his fall into the dark. His consent to Lúthien's marriage and his compassion for the family of Húrin, which is perhaps the only light in that tragedy, give evidence of his largeness of mind and spirit.

Nonetheless, as time goes on, both Thingol's mind and spirit become increasingly dark. And here again is paradox, for the agent of this darkening is the Silmaril, although the cause is within Thingol. The beauty of the jewel quickens the greed already manifest in him. In succumbing to the desire to possess the jewel, and thus the light, Thingol, like Fëanor before him, shows his inability to understand the nature and purpose of light. As the years pass, Thingol becomes increasingly obsessed with the Silmaril. In the words of the narrative, Thingol becomes "bound to it, and he liked not to let it rest even behind the doors of his inmost treasury; and he was minded now to bear it with him always, waking and sleeping" (*TS*, p. 232). The lesson is clear, as it was with Fëanor: the possessor becomes the possessed; the holder of the jewel is caught and held by it.

The likeness between the Silmarils and the One Ring of Sauron, at least in their effects, is striking. Comparison between the two is almost inevitable. Given that, chronologically, the Silmarils were Tolkien's first creation, and must to some extent have affected his treatment of the Ring, the likeness between the two still serves to point up the essential differences, differences which are central to Tolkien's purpose in inventing each. Both the Silmarils and the Ring are artifacts beautiful in themselves and intrinsically desirable. The effect of each is intensified by proximity and possession, and each has an effect proportional to the power and nature of the holder. But there the likenesses end. The Ring is inherently evil, made by evil for evil purposes. It works on the inner darkness of the individual with consistent effect—it can only corrupt. While it appears to confer power on the possessor, in reality the Ring gains power over him. Power, potency, *potentia*—the Ring is all potential for evil, bringing out that potential in the wearer as it brings out all the greed and covetousness inherent in human nature.

The Silmarils are light, pure and simple (in the literal as well as the rhetorical sense). They are holy jewels, light shining in darkness. They exert no power over the wearer; they simply bring out whatever qualities are there to begin with. Where the Ring binds ("One Ring to bring them all, and in the darkness bind them"), the Silmarils illuminate. They can show up darkness if it is there, but they can also call forth light. No wearer can escape the evil power of the Ring, but those who touch a Silmaril can be positively affected if their motives are good.

The Silmaril reveals a clear difference between Beren and Thingol. Beren's quest for the jewel is in its nature unselfish, since he does not want it for itself but as something which will help him to the light, to Lúthien. The Silmaril is the object of the quest, but Lúthien is the subject. Since he has no desire for the Silmaril but only for light as manifest in Lúthien, Beren can touch and hold the jewel without harm, whereas the light has burned Morgoth and will burn the wolf and the sons of Fëanor, who try to take it wrongfully. The image of Beren's hand holding the Silmaril is the emblem of this story, a picture whose power lies as much in what it negates as in what it affirms. Every other hand described as grasping the jewel is burned, but Beren can grasp it precisely because he is not grasping in the metaphorical sense, because he does not want it. (The image of the hand, and especially the hand maimed or cut off, is a frequent motif in Tolkien's fiction. It suggests sacrifice and the ability to give up rather than to get. Beren loses his hand to the wolf, an episode recalling the story of the Norse god Tyr, who sacrificed his hand to bind the wolf Fenrir. Frodo loses his finger to a metaphorical wolf, Gollum, in his sacrifice of himself to overcome evil.)

Beren's hand holding the Silmaril becomes "as a shining lamp," a vehicle for transmitting light. When that hand is bitten off by the wolf Carcharoth, who wants the Silmaril, the power of the jewel in his innards drives him mad with pain. When the wolf is killed and his body ripped open, his belly is burned and consumed, but Beren's hand, holding the Silmaril, is still whole and "incorrupt" (*TS*, p. 186). The word *incorrupt* has a double force here. Beren's hand has not physically decayed; his mortal flesh has not corrupted, even though it has been bitten off and swallowed by the wolf. But his hand is also morally incorruptible; it is a force for good, not to be perverted or brought low.

With Thingol it is otherwise. His desire for the Silmaril is selfish, as Fëanor's grew to be. He wants it for himself only, does not want to share it, and so identifies with it that he keeps it with him at all times. Likewise, Fëanor so identified with the Silmarils that he forgot that the light within them was not his, not made by him. In describing Thingol as *bound* to the Silmaril, Tolkien uses the same word he uses to describe the Ring's purpose—"One Ring to bind." The difference lies in the two forms of the verb: one is active, the other passive. The Ring binds, acts on, anyone who touches it.* Thingol becomes bound not by the jewel but by his own greed.

The Ring activates whatever darkness is latent in the wearer, no matter how hard he may try to fight it. The cardinal example of this is Frodo, whose motive in taking the

---

*Tom Bombadil, on whom the Ring has no effect, is a natural force, a kind of earth spirit, and so the power over the will which the Ring exerts simply has no meaning for him.

Ring is unselfish to the point of self-sacrifice. He does not want the Ring, and tries on two occasions to give it away. Nonetheless, he must eventually succumb to its power. The Silmaril is altogether different, for its effect is wholly determined by the character of the possessor in free reaction to the character of the jewel. The Silmaril is a test, bringing out whatever qualities of light or dark, good or evil, may be present in those who touch it. Response to it is an index of spiritual potential and receptivity to light.

Thus the difference between Beren and Thingol is exemplified only by their differing attitudes toward the Silmaril. Beren is truly drawn to the light, whereas Thingol has manifested a tendency to turn away, to settle for less, from his first appearance in the history. Although a Calaquendi, an Elf of the Light, he moves toward the dark. He exchanges the light of the Trees for the reflected light of Melian; he exchanges Quenya for Sindarin; he exchanges Lúthien for a Silmaril. Over the years his brightness dims, greys, and becomes darkness, a darkness paradoxically intensified by his possession of a Silmaril, and contrasted with its light.

The ultimate hope mixed with Tolkien's predominantly dark vision of human life on earth is manifest in his accounts of the deaths of Beren, Lúthien, and Thingol. Two of the deaths, those of Beren and Lúthien, carry a message of qualified hope, while Thingol's death has no redeeming brightness. Each death is related to the other two, and each death is the fitting culmination for the character, of all that has gone before, the last most typical act. The deaths of Beren and Lúthien run counter to the pattern of death decreed for the race of each. Beren's spirit does not leave the world after his death, but waits in the halls of Mandos for Lúthien. Without Beren, even though she is elven and deathless, Lúthien chooses to die. But both are given a qualified and limited resurrection. They return to Middle-earth to live there as mortals, both subject to a second death.

In thus joining her life to the lives and deaths of men, Lúthien goes against the path of her elven race. But through darkness and death both she and Beren come to the light. In their union a new race is born—the half-elven—who can choose the destiny of either race, and with them comes new hope for both races. Tolkien has called the story of Beren and Lúthien "the Lay of Leithian," Release from Bondage, and the key to his meaning is in the last word. Release from bondage to the circles of the world comes with death, not with so-called immortality. Through death, men can let go; in their deathlessness, elves cannot. The half-elven can also be released from bondage, freed from the earth, if they wish. Tolkien's text makes no promises; what's to come is still unsure. There are no guarantees of a future beyond death; all must be accepted in faith. But this is Tolkien's point. The ability to let go, to trust, is the ability to have faith. To cling to the known, the tangible—even if it is a Silmaril—is to be bound. The deathless elves are, in Tolkien's world, exemplars of wrongful bondage to life undying. Not unlike Swift's Struldbrugs, they are a more attractive but no less powerful lesson in the folly of not letting go.

Thingol exemplifies this folly. He will not leave Middle-earth; he will not let go of Lúthien; and his final inability to let go of the Silmaril brings about his death. When he commissions the dwarves to make their great necklace, Nauglamír, into a setting for the Silmaril, he brings about a work of unique beauty, uniting the greatest works of elves and dwarves. But in doing this he also sets up a fateful clash between his greed and theirs. The dwarves desire the Silmaril, and when he denies it to them, they kill him. Thingol has traveled far—from the light of the Trees to the darkness of the caves where the dwarves have their smithies. His path has been a long one, both in terms of time and in terms of the length of his spiritual regression. He dies in the dark. His last sight is of the Silmaril, the last of the light, but a light no longer accessible to him because of his very possession of it. The darkness of his death works on several levels. He is literally in the dark, deep in the underground caves. Metaphorically, his mind and his vision have been darkened so that he cannot see himself clearly. And spiritually he has withdrawn from the light. He has gone against it and misunderstood it, so that he no longer sees by it or knows how to live in it.

The paradox of the relationship between elves and men lies in the fact that Thingol, just as much as Finrod or Lúthien or Gelmir and Arminas, is responsible for helping men toward the light. Paralleling in his actions the words of Gelmir and Arminas to Tuor, he has set Beren's feet on the road, although he is not able to guide him far. In their path toward the light Beren and Lúthien go through several kinds of darkness. They are separated from one another; they enter the dark strongholds of Sauron and Morgoth, and do battle with their dark minds; they put on darkness—the guises of werewolf and vampire bat—in their quest for the Silmaril. But all these darknesses are part of their path because of the dark action of Thingol's mind in devising the quest. In a very real sense the greatest darkness they pass through is Thingol's own darkness, darkness into which he falls and out of which they emerge. But the actions of all three are tied together, so tangled that they cannot be separated. So, too, are the results of those actions, the apparent good and the apparent evil so mixed that only in the end of the story, at the end of Tolkien's world, will the relationship of each to each be made clear.

What is clear, even this early in the history, is that elves need men as much as men need elves. Elves, going toward darkness, are to set men's feet on the path to the light. With that accomplished, men, less visibly great than elves but with immeasurably greater potential, may be able to turn and help elves come back into the light. The blending of the best of both races in the half-elven race is itself a light in the darkness. It may be that this indwelling light, inherent in the descendants of elves who have seen the light and the descendants of men who are struggling blindly toward it, is now to replace the tangible, external light which was present at the beginning. In Tolkien's world, as in our own, it is only through darkness that one may come to the light.

VII
ONE FRAGMENT

. . . he is rather a study of a hobbit broken by a burden of fear and horror—broken down, and in the end made into something quite different.

TOLKIEN IN A LETTER TO HUGH BROGAN

Where does *The Lord of the Rings* fit into this complex and continuing history? From all accounts it did not begin as part of it, but was started as "the new Hobbit" in response to a request by Tolkien's publishers for another children's book after they had turned down The Silmarillion as unpublishable. But it rapidly became drawn into the older material—older both within and without the myth, in respect to Tolkien's own chronology of composition and as stories of the Elder Days. Only the first chapter echoes the tone of *The Hobbit,* and even that more and more faintly. By the second chapter, "The Shadow of the Past," the story is firmly ensconced within the older myth, and carries it forward. The chapter title itself re-introduces the light/dark motif and tells the reader that what has gone before will darken and affect what is happening now.

The Lord of the Rings is not a children's book in the sense that *The Hobbit* is a children's book, not directed at children nor designed primarily to interest them. But it is certainly literature for children as the Bible is literature for children—and Greek myth, Norse myth, and The Silmarillion—if by that is meant simply-told stories of gods and men, of the human community struggling to find a workable existence in the ebb and surge of forces beyond control and beyond understanding. What gives *The Lord of the Rings* its immediacy, its poignance, and its power to move the reader is Tolkien's combination of the high and far-off times, a great and god-imbued past, with the ordinary, down-to-earth reality of the little man.

The fact that hobbits were no part of Tolkien's original conception makes no matter. That they were born of an idly scribbled phrase across an exam paper—"in a hole in the ground there lived a hobbit"—and that they found their way into the mythology almost by accident is irrelevant to their function within it and to their value as part of the picture. If Tolkien's story of the Fall is a story of man's separation from Light, from God, and if that separation continues and proliferates through fragmentation of light, language, and peoples, then the final working out of the principle will be within the smallest fragments—and appropriately within the smallest people.

The story of the Silmarils proper ends with the disposition of the three jewels, one each in earth, sea, and air. Only the last is visible, that remaining splinter of unsullied light which becomes the evening and morning star, Eärendil. This is the last beacon of hope, the last fragment now set beyond the reach of hands, beyond the possessiveness of human nature. But the exploration of humankind's relationship to light continues. Integral to it is the action through the years of men separated from the light and often from one another, struggling blindly to do right in a darkened, confused, and uncertain world. Nowhere in this continuing history of great deeds and great heroes does Tolkien touch the heart more surely than with the combination in *The Lord of the Rings* of a great task and a little man.

However hobbits arose in Tolkien's imagination, they became, by the last chapters of *The Lord of the Rings*, a necessary part of the myth. Their stature as little people makes them the ideal embodiment of the common man and suggests, among other things, separation by physical type. Hobbits are a splinter folk—clearly of the same stock as men but just as clearly half their size, and therefore a distinction within a whole concept. These unshod little people are closer to the earth than men, more physically in touch with it, more obviously in tune with it. The Gaffer, whose speciality is roots, Farmer Maggot, with "earth under his old feet, and clay on his fingers," Sam, with his shrewd common sense—these are the stuff of the earth. Unexalted, not consciously heroic, hobbits do their jobs, one of which, as Elrond Halfelven says, is to move the wheels of the world while the eyes of the great are elsewhere.

Through hobbits more than any other of Tolkien's peoples, the reader sees himself—his pleasures, sorrows, weaknesses, and strengths. In all Middle-earth, hobbits are best fitted to embody Tolkien's feelings about his fellowmen and the good and bad that happens to them. In Tolkien's fallen world, much of what happens to them is predictably bad. As the process of separation and diminution continues its course, it leads inevitably to yet further fragmentation, to the separation of the individual from society and to what may be the last separation of all—that of the individual from himself. Seen in the context of The Silmarillion, what happens to Frodo is a logical part of the progression, for his is a story of just such separation and dissolution. Tragic in the context of *The Lord of the Rings*, it is still more tragic as the continuation of The Silmarillion. Yet Frodo's fragmentation and alienation from society and self anticipate, however faintly, the final reunion of man with God. The arc can only curve a certain distance away from the starting point before it rounds on itself and begins the return journey. Tolkien takes Frodo to the farthest reach of the arc and leaves him, so there is nowhere to go but back.

While *The Lord of the Rings* encompasses many themes and a chessboard of actions, it is first and foremost Frodo's story, and this gives the book its poignance and its power to move the reader. For the separation which Frodo undergoes from his world and from himself is all too recognizable as the malaise of modern man; in him we experience ourselves. And in light of the larger *mythos* we can understand that this is no discrete phenomenon but part of a continuum which is only complete in that context.

As Frodo's story unfolds, the reader sees two things happening to him, happening as a corollary to, but not as a function of, his adventures. First, as the book progresses, Frodo gradually comes apart, his nature splitting into light and dark. We see this process externally embodied in his relationship with Gollum and even more in Gollum's relationship with himself. Second, Frodo fades, entering more and more into the other-world of the Ring, where the bright light of day dims to grey and only shadows are clear and sharp. Both the splitting and the fading are recapitulations of the process going on in light and language. Frodo is the microcosm, the smallest particle in whom the whole drama of splintering and diminution can be re-enacted. As such he implies the whole, as the grain of sand implies the desert or a mote of dust the round earth.

The story is a journey both literally and metaphorically, and in each case the direction has a meaning beyond the specifically contextual. The pattern of movement which began with the Exile of the Noldor, that great elven sweep out of the light, is now turning back on itself. Those of the Noldor who are left are returning to Aman. They are Calaquendi and have seen the light, and even though the light is gone, Aman is still a holy place. Frodo's doom is to go against this tide and against the westward impulse of men, to go east into the dark. Little evidence of true light remains in Middle-earth, and what there is seems distant from men and their affairs. Sun and moon rise and set; stars shine far away against the night sky. Those stars, the most brilliant of which is Eärendil with the Silmaril on his brow, are all that is left of the light of the Trees. Sauron, the Dark Lord, rules with increasing scope and power, and with the departure of the last Elves of the Light, his darkness is spreading over the world. Some islands of light remain—Rivendell, Lórien, perhaps even the Shire—but they are surrounded by gathering darkness. No great perception is needed to see in this picture the little circle of light Tolkien described in the *Beowulf* essay, that light from which one must venture forth into the surrounding dark. Tolkien recognizes two kinds of darkness—internal and external. Exemplified in his essay by the dragon and Grendel respectively, both darknesses appear in *The Lord of the Rings*, less precisely delineated but still recognizable in the external forces of Sauron and the human internal corruptibility embodied in Gollum.

And of course there is the Ring, that external/internal darkness which has invaded the Shire and is working silently within the little circle of light, working silently on the latent darkness in all human nature. In accepting the Ring, Frodo takes on all that it embodies in its power over inner darkness. In journeying eastward into Mordor, Frodo goes widdershins, against the light for the light's sake. His journey into the dark takes him away from everything he knows and holds dear, including himself. For Frodo's other journey is into his own darkness. He must meet and acknowledge his unadmitted self, that Grendel-like prowler in the wilderness of his psyche which Jung calls the Shadow. In Frodo's case the Shadow is Gollum, who bodies forth with horrible and pitiable clarity the darkness which the Ring evokes. Gollum, a brilliantly realized character, a double self of "I" and "we," of Slinker and Stinker, of Sméagol and Gollum, is Frodo turned inside out. He is also the emblem of Frodo's growing division from himself, a division which we do not see in its proper place until his arrival at the Cracks of Doom. Where Frodo goes against the light because he has to, Gollum turns from the light because he wants to. Light of sun and moon are hateful, even painful to him. He is nocturnal, a creature of night and nightmare, an image out of the unconscious forced into the light of day to be confronted and recognized. And Frodo, who at first refuses to believe that Gollum is a hobbit, comes at last to recognize and pity him. Gollum is both horribly human and horribly hobbit-like.

That Frodo's defeat in Mordor is turned into a kind of victory by Gollum himself does not lessen its bleakness. Here is no *eucatastrophe*, no consolation giving a glimpse of joy. What occurs instead is *katastrophe*, the downward turn when the hero is overcome. The *Beowulf* essay, not the essay on fairy-stories, provides the mood for this part of the story. It needs but little to see in the climactic scene at the Cracks of Doom Tolkien's own version of the Germanic victory of the monsters, to see in Tolkien's Middle-earth Beowulf's *eormengrund*, the great earth ringed with *garsecg*, the shoreless sea, to see in Frodo all those heroes who, with courage as their stay, went forward to that battle with the offspring of the dark which ends for all in defeat.

The outcome of the battle is defeat—for Frodo as for

Beowulf—but the nature of the struggle and the terms of the defeat are Tolkien's own and peculiarly a product of his age. For all its mythic timelessness, Tolkien's work could only have been written in and for the twentieth century. The work draws on many myths for its truth, but it speaks directly to an age acutely concerned with the workings of its own unconscious, an age comfortable—or uncomfortable—with psychology, familiar with the concepts and terminology of Freud and Jung. Inevitably, the journey, the battle, and the monster are all within as well as without. The outcome of the struggle is a blend of Germanic heroism, Jungian psychology, and Christian sacrifice. Frodo's decision to keep the Ring—an act of free will—is a recapitulation of the Fall of Adam; his possessive need for the Ring is an echo of Melkor, of Fëanor, of Thingol. The whole episode is Tolkien's extended gloss on the nature of the Fall.

For the Fall is separation—from God, from the Light, from wholeness of self and world. In this sense Frodo is more than emblematic of fallen man; he is archetypal. His encounter with Gollum, his shadow, his Grendel, is emblematic of the growing division of self within him. Emblematic, too, is his destination—the Cracks of Doom—carrying in its name a concept of crack-up, of coming apart, and embodying in its volcanic nature his inner turmoil. Without overt psychologizing, Tolkien shows in a series of vivid scenes Frodo's struggle against darkness and division of self.

Two scenes stand out sharply, pictured moments that mark the boundaries of Frodo's psychological and spiritual journey inward. The first is the moment in the high seat at Amon Hen when, caught between the contending wills of Sauron and Gandalf, he takes off the Ring. The second is at the Cracks of Doom when he puts the Ring on. Dramatically, psychologically, and thematically, the first scene prepares for the second:

> The two powers strove in him. For a moment, perfectly balanced between their piercing points, he writhed, tormented. Suddenly he was aware of himself again, Frodo, neither the Voice nor the Eye; free to choose and with

one remaining instant in which to do so. He took the
Ring off his finger. (*LOTR*, I, p. 519)

A great deal is going on here. The first thing to notice is
the preposition; the powers strive *in* him, not over him or
about him. He is the battlefield, and while the powers are
external forces it seems clear that they are also aspects of his
nature. Externally they are Sauron, the Dark Lord, and Gandalf, no longer the Grey but the White. But within Frodo they
are simply the light and dark of his own nature. Thus pin-
ioned between light and dark both inside and outside, Frodo
is perfectly balanced and tormented by the equal stress of
positive and negative forces. He is neither one nor the other,
nor yet both. He is not Frodo, but the force field of opposing
poles. His release comes when he is aware of *himself* again,
aware as an independent being with a will of his own—when
he is free to choose.

It is otherwise at the Cracks of Doom. There Frodo,
weakened by his long journey and his wounds, finally broken
by his burden, succumbs to the force of darkness. Working
on the growing darkness within him, the Ring has eroded his
will so that he is no longer *himself*. He is separated from his
true being and has become what Gollum has so dreadfully
embodied. Frodo's words as he sets the Ring on his finger are
filled with awful irony: " 'I do not choose' " and " 'I will not
do' " (*LOTR*, III, p. 274). His use of "will" and "choose" makes
it clear that he believes that he is acting freely. But the negative, the repeated "not," is telling evidence that his will has
been perverted and his choice pre-empted.

The moment is shocking and powerful; the mind wants
to reject it. It is unthinkable that the best hobbit of them all
should go bad after his long struggle, his sacrifice, and the
humility and the mercy he has shown. It is a triumph of evil.
Having engineered such a shock, Tolkien, with consummate
dramatic timing, shifts the spotlight to Gollum, shows his
reaction to Frodo—more overwhelming than the reader's—
and brings the scene to its close with the triumph of evil
undoing itself.

What has happened has happened. It was not destined,

not necessarily foresung in the Music, and yet the concatenation of events is such that nothing else could have happened. The Ring is governed by fate, its very creation foreshadowed in the Music. Gollum and Frodo, each of the race of men, have the power to act beyond the Music and to have their actions shape events. Tolkien describes the destruction of the Ring and the salvation of Frodo as "grace," the unforeseeable result of actions by Sam, Frodo, and Gollum:

> [Gollum] did rob and injure [Frodo] in the end—but by a 'grace', that last betrayal was at a precise juncture when the final evil deed was the most beneficial thing anyone cd. have done for Frodo! (*TLOT,* p. 234)

Fate and free will have come together to produce the unpredictable, necessary, and inevitable end.

But nothing is ever ended—in this world. Standing at the brink, Sam sees Frodo, rid of the Ring, raped of his finger, once again "the dear master of the sweet days in the Shire" (*LOTR,* III, p. 276). This is wishful thinking. The view is through Sam's eyes, and Sam is blinded by love and hope. Frodo is not the same, nor will he be, for he has failed. He is broken, maimed, less than whole by more than the loss of his finger or even the loss of the Ring. He has lost the self he once was. He offered himself for a purpose, was used, and buckled under the weight; the Ring-bearer was not equal to the burden. His creator describes him as "broken by a burden of fear and horror." But Tolkien also says he is broken down— "broken down, and in the end made into something quite different." This enlarges the picture, for "broken down" means something more and something other than "broken." To be broken down can mean to be broken and unable to function, as a piece of machinery breaks down. But it can also mean to be taken apart, to be separated into components as light is refracted or broken down by a prism. Broken down in this sense, fragmented, Frodo can, without ever being other than himself, stand for all the fragmentation in Tolkien's world. He is the smallest common denominator, the least splinter. He is the mote.

The metaphor here is of light whole and light refracted,

of the Logos fragmented into the *verbum,* of the world of Middle-earth broken so that it can be re-made, to "Man, finally redeemed" and thus "like and unlike the fallen that we know." Tolkien deals with the first part of the process but withholds the second. He shows Frodo fallen, but barely adumbrates his redemption and re-making, a treatment that is consistent with his view of history as a long defeat. While he may describe Frodo as "in the end made into something quite different," the story merely shows him sick, unhappy, uneasy, and out of place in what was once his home. At the end of the book he takes a ship for the Undying Lands to be healed—if he can be. Tolkien is careful to leave even that open to question:

> Frodo was sent or allowed to pass over Sea to heal him—if that could be done, *before he died.* He would have eventually to 'pass away': no mortal could, or can, abide for ever on earth, or within Time. So he went both to a purgatory and to a reward, for a while: a period of reflection and peace and a gaining of a truer understanding of his position in littleness and in greatness. ... (*TLOT,* p. 328)

Frodo's littleness is clear, as is his greatness in terms of his sacrifice. But greatness in terms of what he may become, the "something quite different," is not shown. There is no Recovery, no Consolation, no glimpse of Joy beyond the walls of the world. Tolkien does not take Frodo that far. The only hint at apotheosis is withheld from the end, tucked away in a little incident early in the story, at the opening of Book Two of *The Fellowship.* And hint it is, the merest of allusions to things past, present, and (possibly) future.

At Rivendell, Gandalf pays a bedside visit to Frodo, who is recuperating from his fight at Weathertop, his dash to the Ford, and his defiance of the Ringwraiths. Although he insists that he is recovering, Frodo shows the effects of his knife-wound and the burden of the Ring. The wizard notices

> a faint change, just a hint as it were of transparency about him, and especially about the left hand that lay outside upon the coverlet.

> 'Still that must be expected,' said Gandalf to him-
> self, 'he is not half through yet, and to what he will
> come in the end not even Elrond can foretell. Not to
> evil, I think. He may become like a glass filled with
> clear light for eyes to see that can.' (*LOTR*, I, p. 295)

Here, too, a great deal is going on, for the references to
transparency, to the light-filled glass, reach beyond the immediate context. On the face of it, and in the context of *The
Lord of the Rings* only, the hint of transparence suggests that
Frodo is fading because of his contact with evil, because of
the wound from the Morgul-knife and his continuing contact
with the Ring. And this is, of course, the case, although it is
not the whole story. One of the effects of the Ring is to make
the wearer "fade." To wear it for invisibility brings down
some sort of cumulative and lasting effect, as if each trip into
the invisible robs the wearer of some concrete reality. Thus
Frodo is fading out of the everyday world. Already he is more
than a little inside the other-world of the Ring, where he is
visible to evil and it is more visible to him than the every-
dayness of his real world. Tolkien has prepared for this in his
picture of the Ringwraiths, shadows of evil, and in Aragorn's
horrified reaction to Frodo's little joke about getting so thin
that he will become a wraith.

But this is not just about wraiths and shadows—it is
about light and appearance. To become invisible, however
helpful it may be for playing pranks on dwarves or avoiding
the Sackville-Bagginses, is to negate the effects of light. It is
to deal in dis-appearances rather than appearances. It is the
negative—not the opposite—of "to shine." To be invisible is
to be neither light nor dark. In terms of light it is not to be
at all. Thus Frodo is losing his physical self. In the specific
context of his life and his journey what is happening to him
is not good, but in the ultimate context of what Tolkien envisions as man's final end it may lead to good. Light no longer
reveals the external Frodo, and within him light and dark are
at war. But when the battle is over, and dark has won and
destroyed itself and left the field, his transparency, his lack
of appearance, may go beyond mere fading to transcend ma-
teriality altogether. He is being emptied so that he may be

filled with clear light, so that the White Light which held the mote may now be held within the mote, to shine "for eyes to see that can."

Gandalf's auxiliary verb is important. He does not say Frodo will become, or must become—he says Frodo may become. This is speculation, not prediction. *May*, Old English *magan*, "to be able," describes capacity, not actuality. What Gandalf sees is potential in Frodo; he may or he may not realize it. As the Music is the potential for the world that is, this capacity to become is the potential of the Frodo that is. If it is realized, it will come out of Frodo's willingness to be subsumed into a greater cause than himself. Through his own actions, the sacrifice of himself in which he lets himself be used for good and broken by the power of evil, he may paradoxically be redeemed by his own failure. With a degree of self-abnegation matched only by Gandalf's surrender of himself in Moria, Frodo goes beyond evil, beyond self, beyond physical or mental wholeness to be completely broken down that he may be re-made. He is splintered light, and in his fragmentation he makes obvious the need for re-union with self, with world, and with God that Tolkien feels is Joy beyond the walls of the world. He will not get back what he has lost, but he may get something else and more. He will be in the end "made into something quite different," for as Tolkien says of man's longing for Eden, "We shall never recover it, for that is not the way of repentance, which works spirally and not in a closed circle; we may recover something like it, but on a higher plane" (*TLOT*, p. 110).

The image of Frodo broken down, a small splinter of light, invites comparison with the book's other image of white broken into the color spectrum—Saruman the White, who renames himself Saruman of many Colours, whose robes, "which had seemed white, were not so, but were woven of all colours, and if he moved they shimmered and changed hue so that the eye was bewildered" (*LOTR*, I, p. 339). When Gandalf comments that he likes white better, Saruman replies sneeringly, " 'The white light can be broken.' " Gandalf answers, " 'In which case it is no longer white. And he that breaks a thing to find out what it is has left the path of wisdom' " (*LOTR*, I, p. 339). Saruman, in his pride, has broken himself, not by yielding to a cause greater than himself but by trying to impose himself upon the cause, by endeavoring to control rather than to let himself be used. Instead of accepting his position—the very opposite of Frodo's—of greatness and littleness, he has traded his greatness for the wrong kind of littleness. The pettiness engendered by swollen pride, rather than the humble realization of littleness, differentiates Saruman from Frodo. Frodo knows how small he is. He knows, too, how unfitted he is for the task—he is not made for perilous quests—and he recognizes that he does not know how to achieve the end: " 'I will take the Ring, though I do not know the way,' " he says (*LOTR*, I, p. 354). Saruman, in the inflation of his precious self, knows a little but thinks he knows more, and that it is enough. But he does not know, and does not realize he does not know. Thus a world of difference separates him from Frodo.

With regard to the light, the closest parallel to Frodo is not another character but the light itself, most closely linked to him in the Phial of Galadriel. The light has been divided just as Frodo becomes divided, broken down just as he is gradually broken down. Yet as fragments both Frodo and the light have a purpose, and each must follow its own nature. While Frodo goes against the light, he also carries it with him, finding his way into the darkness by the last splinter of the true light. When the book is read in the context of The Silmarillion, the references to light, and particularly starlight, scattered throughout the story assume coherence. And of all aspects of light, the Phial of Galadriel is the most important. The Phial, Galadriel's gift to Frodo as the company leaves Lórien, is the light of Eärendil caught in the waters of her fountain. It is the light of the last Silmaril, the last splinter of the light of Aman given to the eyes of Middle-earth.

A pattern of balance and opposition links the Phial to Frodo and to the Ring. The Ring is the story's all-important object; its darkness is so powerful and pervasive that no equally powerful counterbalance is immediately perceivable. Nevertheless, the Ring is balanced, as are all forces in the story, by an opposite, and it is the Phial. As the Ring is the cause of Frodo's journey, so the Phial is his beacon. As Galadriel's gift, it matches the Ring, so often referred to as a "present." As light, it balances the Ring's darkness. It is meant to be carried in the hand, contained within it, whereas the Ring is to be worn, and must contain its wearer.

Both Frodo and the Phial are fragments—Frodo of humanity, the Phial of the light. Both are momentarily caught and held by Galadriel; both are sent on their way by her. Galadriel, who gives the Phial, has seen the light and has left it behind. Frodo, who receives it, is afraid of the dark but is going into it. And finally, the Phial as it is—a glass filled with clear light—is in its being what Frodo may attain in his becoming. It anticipates his future.

But so does the Ring, and here Tolkien's pattern of coming to light through darkness is at its most immediate and powerful. The Ring and the Phial define Frodo; he must succumb to one before he can have the hope of becoming like the other. He carries both with him on his journey—the one to light his path to the unmaking of the other. Here the next thread joins the pattern and reverses it. For in all Tolkien's great account of sub-creation, *The Lord of the Rings* is the one story which is about un-making, not making. The whole pattern of sub-creating, of splintering and separating and dividing, comes to a sudden halt in the total destruction of Gollum and the Ring. In this last separation Frodo is separated from himself and from his darkness at a point where that very darkness causes itself to un-be. Un-making is the corollary of making, and equally important. In the fallen world which Tolkien has envisioned, such breakdown is inevitable. It is the next step in the process, and as such is both result and cause, predicated on all that has gone before, the basis for what is still to come. It is the leaf mold of creation.

As the Ring is unmade, so Frodo is unmade, broken down so that he may be transformed. But Tolkien's story ends here. We know what may happen but not what will happen to Frodo, no more than we know what will happen to us. Tolkien has said that he conceived his whole mythology to illustrate the necessity of accepting "Hope without guarantees" (*TLOT*, p. 237). This, and the gateway to that hope—death—

are the gifts of Ilúvatar, God's gift to men. They are precarious gifts, hard to trust, hard to appreciate. For it is hard, as Tolkien well knew, to let go—to let go of one's treasure, let go of one's self, let go of the world. Hope without guarantees gives little hint of what comes after. Salvation and redemption and the Music played aright may be alluded to, but they are not shown.

Tolkien has said that his mythology encompasses a Last Battle, a Ragnarøk, and the re-making of the world (*TLOT*, p. 149). It would be strange if he had not, for the myths on which he draws most heavily, Judeo-Christian and Norse, both include re-making and renewal. The Norse myth tells of the children of the gods, and of the return of Baldr, and of a new earth and a new man and woman. The Judeo-Christian myth tells of a new heaven and a new earth, and the heavenly city where the light of God shines and there is no night. But in neither myth does such an account make up one hundredth of the subject matter, because the mythographer is a man whose heart is in the struggle and whose mind is fixed on it—as is Tolkien's. Hope without guarantees is balanced, in the continuing play of light and shadow, by doubt, if not by outright despair.

And so the book ends with Frodo broken but not healed, broken down but not re-made. He is wounded and sick—so much the book tells us—and he will die, as Tolkien's comments make clear. Gandalf's vision in Rivendell does offer some hope for him. But a curious and disturbing poem in *The Tolkien Reader*, rather tenuously linked to Frodo, counters Gandalf's vision with a very different picture. This is altogether outside the book and would go unremarked except that Tolkien has gone out of his way to associate the two. "The Sea-bell" is one of a group of poems included in the *Reader* as part of "The Adventures of Tom Bombadil and other verses." The fictive conceit which unites them is that they are all pieces from the Red Book, some formally included, some scribbled on loose leaves or in margins. A preface in the scholarly voice of the Prologue to *The Lord of the Rings* informs the reader that these verses are "legends and jests of the Shire at the end of the Third Age." Most, we are told, are by unknown authors, probably hobbits, quite possibly Bilbo, his friends, and their descendants. Further, they are "in various hands and were probably written down from oral tradition."[1] So far they are presented as having some historical as well as literary interest, supporting and extending the range of hobbit-lore, and, of course, adding to the subcreative reality of Middle-earth.

About "The Sea-bell," number fifteen in the collection, the scholar says that it is included "because a hand has scrawled at its head *Frodos Dreme*. That is remarkable," he comments, "and though the piece is unlikely to have been written by Frodo himself, the title shows that it was associated with the dark and despairing dreams which visited him in March and October during his last three years" (*TR*, p. 194). Having tentatively linked the poem to Frodo, he immediately backs off by adding that it may instead be part of "other traditions concerning Hobbits that were taken by the 'wandering madness', and if they ever returned, were afterwards queer and uncommunicable" (*TR*, p. 194).

Like many of the poems in the *Reader*, "The Sea-bell" was originally part of Tolkien's early work, and was not explicitly connected with his mythology. A version first appeared in 1934 in the *Oxford Magazine* under the title "Looney," which may have given rise to the "wandering madness" explanation. Whatever it was or is supposed to be, it draws a picture of such displacement, alienation, and despair as to negate hope, with or without guarantees. But whatever its real origins or its fictive provenance, whether the author is Frodo, someone who knew him, or any wandering hobbit, Tolkien's decision to publish it with the historical and scholarly apparatus added is worth examining as a gauge of his feelings about Frodo's eventual end. For, of course, Tolkien is the poet, the annotator, and the scholar, and it is his judgment which chooses to present conflicting evidence about the poem.

---

[1] J. R. R. Tolkien, *The Tolkien Reader* (New York: Ballantine Books, 1966; rpt. 1979), p. 194. Hereafter page references will be cited parenthetically in the text, with this abbreviation: *TR*.

The nameless speaker in the poem hears a sea-bell call, finds a ship waiting, and is borne over the sea to an unknown destination. There he finds an enchanted country much like Valinor, with glittering, jeweled sands, green hills, and fountains. The traveler climbs a hill and walks through meadows. Although the land is peopled, he can see no one. He hears echoes of song, of voices calling and feet dancing, but silence falls wherever he goes. He calls but gets no answer, and at last, through a dark cloud, he comes to a silent, bare, decaying wood. There he stays—alone—for a year and a day, the traditional time of enchantment. His despairing cry—"I have lost myself, and I know not the way/but let me be gone!"— recalls Frodo at the end of *The Lord of the Rings.* When winter comes, the traveler returns over the sea to the land of men but finds no welcome there, either. "Houses were shuttered, wind round them muttered/roads were empty" (*TR,* pp. 246-247). Caught between Middle-earth and a version of Valinor, he is no part of either world, lost and unacknowledged "as in sad lane/in blind alley and in long street/ragged I walk. To myself I talk/for still they speak not, men that I meet" (*TR,* p. 247).

The situation is recognizable as a variation of the common fairy-tale motif, the Rip van Winkle story of the adventurer who wanders into faërie and returns after an apparently brief time to find himself changed and his world unrecognizable. Its importance to Tolkien's thought is found in the subtitle and the consequent reciprocal effect of the poem and *The Lord of the Rings* on one another. Whatever its merits as a poem—Auden called it "wonderful" (*TLOT,* p. 378)— "The Sea-bell" provokes speculation on the possible state of mind of Frodo, if it is Frodo, and even more on the possible state of mind of the author, for whether the speaker is Frodo or not, it is certainly Tolkien. If the speaker is Frodo, then the reader is being told that he sees himself as irrecoverably lost, condemned to a half-life which is not life at all, suspended between two worlds, that his sacrifice has led to no redemption. And something in Tolkien wants the reader to hear Frodo in the poem, to link the situation with what becomes of Frodo. We may speculate that Tolkien hears in it

Frodo's voice, and that behind Frodo's voice he hears his own, for he could only envision this end for Frodo if he could envision it for himself. Carpenter's comment on Tolkien's feelings after his mother's death may be apropos: nothing is safe, nothing will last, no battle will be won forever.

The same conflict of moods that has marked Tolkien's work from the first is apparent here. The combination of the poem and its scholarly apparatus permits Tolkien to say a number of things and at the same time call them into question. It may be Frodo's dream and then again it may not be. It may be no one's dream, but simply a dark and hopeless vision which somebody else has rightly or wrongly assigned to Frodo because its bleakness evokes Frodo's troubled state in his last years. Behind all this fiction lies the truth of the author's inner conflict. Behind the multiplicity of personas is the man who is all of them, who has conflicting things to say and chooses to say them in conflicting voices. One voice, however, the primary voice of the speaker in the poem, is recognizable to the careful reader as the same voice that questioned the existence of God in a letter to his son.

The dream concept suggested by the secondary voice is important, for it associates the poem with the medieval convention of the dream-vision, the function of which is to imply that truth beyond observable reality is being revealed to the dreamer, and through him to the reader. As a medievalist, Tolkien was, of course, thoroughly familiar with this; he knew the dream-reality of Langland's *Piers Plowman* and Chaucer's *Book of the Duchess*, as well as the mad logic and modern surreality of Lewis Carroll's "Alice" books. He knew that dream is powerfully effective both as real experience and as literary device, for in each case it bypasses rational intellect to speak directly from the unconscious to the waking mind. Man has always found meaning in dreams, knowing, as Tolkien knew, that "in dreams strange powers of the mind may be unlocked" (*TR*, p. 41)

And so to call "The Sea-bell" *Frodos Dreme* is to invest it with truth, to give it validity as a vision of another reality beyond the merely real. But the temptation to accept it as Tolkien's last word is hampered by two considerations. First, the unknown hand is only one comment on the poem, and Tolkien deliberately leaves it obscure. He may be hiding behind the obscurity, or he may intend it to discount the poem's importance. Second, the dream (if it is a dream) is balanced and opposed by another dream, which gives a different and considerably more hopeful picture. This other is Frodo's last dream in the house of Tom Bombadil, a vision given added force by its repetition at the end of the book as the culmination of his last voyage: "And then it seemed to him that as in his dream in the house of Bombadil, the grey rain-curtain turned all to silver glass and was rolled back, and he beheld white shores and beyond them a far green country under a swift sunrise" (*LOTR*, III, p. 384).

This, too, is dream, but it is dream come true, made real by waking experience. And so where are we? What, in Tolkien's view, has really happened to Frodo? It seems clear that there is no single final answer; rather, as is so often the case with this complex and seemingly contradictory author, beneath the surface lies the simple truth that he does not know, that hope and desire are balanced by despair, and that the final vision remains a vision only, called into question by his hard-won knowledge of the dark, given affirmation by his continuing faith.

VIII
ONE GOOD
CUSTOM

The Fall of Man is in the past and far off stage;
the Redemption of Man in the far future.

TOLKIEN IN A LETTER TO 'MR. RANG'

Two ideas central to Tolkien's philosophy emerge with increasing force as the myth is studied. One is the inevitability, indeed, the absolute necessity, of change. The other is the necessity of language and its importance as both agent and tool. These two ideas are linked psychologically, philologically, and spiritually, for each is an aspect of the other. And they are closely tied to Tolkien's history as agents and functions of its design. From change, whether good or bad, benign or cataclysmic, comes growth and development, and one of the chief instruments of change is language, altering and governing perception. Out of change comes new perception, and hence new language. Language separates, distinguishes, and divides, breaking down and refining aspects of original, undifferentiated reality. But it is more than a refiner of meaning; it is also preserver and creator. New concepts, new metaphors, incantatory adjectives can enhance meaning and so re-create reality. Tolkien's mythology is a record of change—change in history, change in language—and of the inevitable result: change in awareness.

Language is the heart of his concept, and the speaker's meaning is crucial to his design. And so the fact that "The Sea-bell" ends with a situation wherein a speaker fails to generate meaning, fails in attempts to communicate with others, is startling and unsettling in the context of his mythology. It seems, moreover, especially poignant as the work of a philologist and inventor of languages. What does he mean by this? How does it fit into his design and his philosophy? The man who wanted to create a world in which the words *elen síla lúmenn' omentielmo* ("A star shines on the hour of our meeting") would be a common greeting (*TLOT*, p. 265) has created a moment in which there is no greeting. A man whose lifework has been predicated on the value of the word, a man whose religion as well as his fiction is founded on the power of the Logos, has envisioned a moment in which the value and power of the word are denied. Communication turns inward on itself and language fails to fulfill its purpose: "To myself I talk; for still they speak not, men that I meet."

Language in Tolkien's world has shaped its users and has been shaped by them, enhancing awareness and growing out of it. But in "The Sea-bell" language has no use, and the awareness thus created—of isolation and separation—is so complete that nothing can bridge it. Cut off wholly from others, talking only to himself and thus both self-defined and self-divided, the speaker has come as far as change and language as he knows them will carry him. He is at the point on the circle most distant from the beginning, the point opposed to it. With awareness of light came the first utterance, the impulse to communicate. Now, in the moment of greatest separation, and thus of greatest awareness and impulse to speech, utterance is useless. The speaker without speech is psychologically and spiritually in the dark. Cut off from earth and shut out of heaven, he has nothing with which to bridge the separation or to light his way. He cannot communicate.

The word itself—*communicate*—is loaded with inherent meaning, meaning that is particularly important to Tolkien, carrying as it does in a single concept the basis of both his profession and his faith. For the idea embodied in communication includes, in both the literal and the metaphorical sense, language and feeling. Without communication of some sort, man is cut off from his community. Without community there is no sense of communion. Without Communion in the highest degree, fallen man is truly cut off, not just from his fellowman but from his God. In its Christian and Catholic meaning, the rite of Communion, the Blessed Sacrament, is the act of atonement, of at-one-ment and re-union with God. It was for Tolkien the most important and meaningful of all the rites of his church. "The only cure for sagging of fainting faith is Communion," he wrote to his son Michael (*TLOT*, p. 338). The statement is straightforward, plain, unequivocal. It is clear evidence of the firmness of his religious feeling. Yet the phrase "fainting faith," addressed to his son's need, testifies to his own understanding of doubt and despair. That Tolkien was well acquainted with fainting faith is suggested by Humphrey Carpenter, who said of him: "When he could not bring himself to go to confession he would deny himself communion and live in a pathetic state of spiritual depression" (*TAB*, p. 128).

No great effort of imagination is required to connect Tolkien's feeling for and about language with his feeling for and about communication—the one is the emblem of the other. Nor is it difficult to compare the state of the speaker at the end of "The Sea-bell" with Tolkien's "state of spiritual depression." And it is safe to speculate that the reverse of both situations would also be comparable. Communion in the religious sense is communication transcended, lifted beyond language to the experience of the unutterable. To communicate with others is to participate in community. To take Communion, to partake of the body and blood of Christ, the Word made flesh, is to participate in God and the Word by means of God and the Word, to be in community with God.

Such an experience involves leaving one state and entering another. It is to be re-formed and re-newed, to be changed. This concept of change is embodied in both *communicate* and *communion*. The obvious philological similarity between the two words suggests a common ancestor and implies an original shared meaning in line with Barfield's concept of original semantic unity. The evidence supports this. Both words derive from Latin *commūnis*, "common," in the sense of "shared by all alike." Both words thus carry some sense of interchange among people or between man and God, giving a sense of community. Change is implicit here, but at the next step back it is explicit. The parent word *commūnis* comes from the compound adjective *ko-moin-i-*, "held in common," which comes from *moi-n-*, the suffixed o-grade form of Indo-European *mei-*[1], "to change, go, move." Clearly, the original concept was one of change, to which the prefix *ko-*, "together," added the idea of change in community, of going or moving toward one another or moving together toward something or someone else.

The laws of movement which govern the macrocosm and the microcosm, the universe and the individual, are laws of change—change of state, of direction, of nature. Just so are the laws which govern Tolkien's world. His Prime Mover, Eru, whose name may be related to Indo-European *er-*[1], "to set in motion," has invested his world with change, with ebb and surge, with advance and retreat, in which the farthest point from the Light, from God, is also the beginning of the journey back.

Tolkien's philosophical and religious outlook was that change is necessary, although his psychological and emotional yearning was for much of his world that had vanished or was vanishing. Both feelings are evident in his work. He mourns the fading of Lórien and the passing of the Entwives. " 'I should be sad,' " says Théoden to Gandalf, " 'for however the fortune of war shall go, may it not so end that much that was fair and wonderful shall pass forever out of Middle-earth?' " And Gandalf replies, " 'It may.' " Then he adds, " 'But to such days we are doomed. Let us now go on with the journey we have begun!' " (*LOTR,* II, p. 197). Both speak for Tolkien, but Gandalf has the last word.

Strongest evidence of Tolkien's certainty about the necessity of change is his invention of the immortal and changeless elves, whom he described as "embalmers" (*TLOT,* p. 197). Their inclination to arrest change is his notion (in fictive theory, if not in practice) of what not to do. "Mere *change* as such," he wrote of his invented world, "is not represented as 'evil': it is the unfolding of the story and to refuse this is of course against the design of God. But the Elvish weakness is in these terms naturally to regret the past, and to become unwilling to face change. . . . They desired some power over things as they are . . . to arrest change, and keep things always fresh and fair" (*TLOT,* p. 236).

Desire to preserve a present good inevitably becomes desire to keep it from passing, but this leads to decay. The process of change is the design of God, and it must continue if the design is to be fulfilled. However good things may be or seem, however bad the future may look, the present inevitably becomes the past. Norse scholar that he was, Tolkien knew the mythic Norse view of time embodied in the names of the Norns, *Urð*, goddess of the past, *Verðandi*, goddess of the present, and *Skuld*, goddess of the future. All three names are verb forms, and *Verðandi* is the present participle of *verða*, "to happen, occur." It is literally "happening" or "becoming," and so characterizes a process, not a state. The present is not a static, discrete thing but a flowing transition. We are always becoming, and to look back with regret, like Lot's wife, is to risk losing the capacity and the will to go forward. "The old order changeth," said Tennyson's Arthur to the regretful Bedivere, "yielding place to new, and God fulfills himself in many ways, lest one good custom should corrupt the world." Tolkien would agree.

Moreover, to try to arrest change is to reject that increase in perception which change must bring. Any change will be internal as well as external, involving what Barfield calls a "felt change of consciousness" (*PD*, p. 52). While his immediate reference is to the experience of poetry, the phrase may legitimately be extended to any experience. For experience is perceived in our appreciation of it, and the appreciation of experience, as Barfield says, depends no more on what is being changed than it does on the change itself. The value of speech is appreciated as it fades into silence, the value of light as it shades into dark, the value of hope as it declines into despair.

And so the speaker in "The Sea-bell" (who may be Frodo, is certainly Tolkien, and is probably all humanity) is important to the myth because he experiences change. He is a man of antitheses, both literally and spiritually a traveler between worlds. His experience of loss makes him appreciate what is lost and know himself as the loser. Although the poem pictures the moment as painful in its loneliness and lonely in its painfulness, the experience of these feelings—the disease—brings with it enhanced awareness. The speaker knows himself precisely because he has lost everything else. And the reader shares the speaker's experience vicariously, gaining through him that felt change of consciousness which is the knowledge of becoming.

If this seems like carrying the poem too far and loading it with more freight than it was designed to carry, it may be worth remembering that the poet also is in transition, caught in the force field between the poles of his hope and his despair. Worth remembering, too, is that he saw his great predecessor and model, the *Beowulf* poet, as a man in transition, moved to creation by the intersection of old belief and new scripture. For transition is of the essence of poetry as it is of the essence of the world from which poetry springs, which poetry seeks to re-create. In this context it would seem valid to see all three men—the speaker in "The Sea-bell," his creator Tolkien, and Tolkien's master, the *Beowulf* poet—as men of antitheses conscious of loss and, through it, conscious of change, vouchsafed only a glimpse of joy, poised at the turn, as yet unable to realize it.

This is Tolkien's fairy-story moment, the "turn," at the moment of becoming. It is reversal, *metanoia,* redemption felt before the mind can grasp it, before the knowledge of the happy ending and the consolation. The moment is precarious, for *katastrophe* is imminent and has not yet become *eucatastrophe.* But if the moment is precarious it is also precious, valuable in and for itself because this is what generates subcreation. If humanity is Frodo in "The Sea-bell," wounded, lost, bereft of paradise and out of sight of heaven, then humanity is aware—painfully aware, perhaps, but able to turn it to use. Man is the maker, the poet, the teller of tales for whom light and language are instruments of sub-creation. Having built gods and their houses out of dark and light and sowed the seed of dragons, man must worship the gods and fight the dragons. And of these, the dragons are the more immediate: "For the monsters do not depart, whether the gods go or come." In this world, in Time, the dragons of the darkness will prevail. And Tolkien, Christian, Roman Catholic, knew that history will never be anything but a long defeat. Still, he had faith that through darkness one might come to the light. Man will lose the battle, lose himself, and lose his life—but he that loses his life shall find it. And in the making of poetry, in the sub-creating of a world man may re-make himself, may carry himself beyond words to the Word and so become the architect, in collaboration with God, of his own redemption.

Collaboration with God is the acknowledged principle behind Tolkien's creative effort. His references to reporting and recording rather than inventing, his allusions to finding out the etymologies of his words rather than making them up clearly indicate that he was aware of something more and other than himself at work. In a letter to a reader of *The Lord of the Rings*, he referred to "The Writer of the Story (by which I do not mean myself)" (*TLOT*, p. 253). Tolkien knew himself to be a poet, and had certifiable confidence in his own abilities and his elvish craft. But he also knew beyond a doubt that he was the prism, not the light. He was the sub-creator, the combiner, the mythical grammarian. Beyond him, working in and through him, he felt the Primary Creator, the Mover, the Initiator of Change. This concept is paralleled within his mythology, wherein all of the sub-creators are in one way or another functions of Eru, weavers of the design as well as threads in it. Any author must be all of his characters, for he must find them in himself in order to put them on paper. But for Tolkien, Eru is not a character and thus no part of himself. He is beyond knowing as God is beyond knowing, beyond identity or identification.

Of the other characters, the one who at first glance would seem to most clearly reflect Tolkien is Aulë, whose creation of the dwarves is an explicit attempt at sub-creation in imitation of his creator. But this effort is abortive, and since Aulë is rebuked for his impulse it does not fit the interlacing of light and word which is so much a part of Tolkien's pattern. Fëanor is also a candidate, but his rebellion and vain pursuit of the light nullify his sub-creative abilities after his first great effort. Of all his characters, the one with whom Tolkien most explicitly identified himself is not a sub-creator at all in the usual sense, for he is not a maker but a lover—Beren, the hero of Tolkien's love story, the lover of Lúthien and the light, the seeker of the Silmaril. In fact, the names of Beren and Lúthien are carved on the stone marking the grave where Tolkien and his wife Edith are buried.

Although Tolkien wrote of his wife that "she was (and knew she was) my Lúthien" (*TAB*, p. 97), and although the meeting of Beren and Lúthien in the wood paralleled Tolkien's memories of early moments in his marriage, Beren must be seen as more than a lover. His role is that of quest-hero, and his adventures come from his identifying love with the light. This invites speculation that Tolkien's identification with Beren is based on the Silmaril as well as Lúthien, and that the two, as well as Beren's relationship to them, are interlocked in Tolkien's vision. Beren alone, of all the men of Middle-earth, is allowed to come to the light through the darkness, to make real the fleeting glimpse of joy and the consolation of the happy ending. He is the antithesis of Frodo, of the speaker in "The Sea-bell," of Tolkien's pull toward the dark. He embodies Tolkien's hope, not his doubt or his despair.

For all the sub-creators who move through The Silmarillion, who work with light and splinter and diffuse it, it is Beren who rescues the light from darkness and brings it back into the world. Without him, although the light would still exist, no one would see it, no one would be guided by it. To identify himself with Beren, Tolkien must have known that however flawed he was, however dark his vision of his world, he too had been allowed to bring a splinter of the light to Middle-earth.

| BIBLIOGRAPHY

Auerbach, Erich. *Mimesis.* Trans. Willard B. Trask. Princeton: Princeton University Press, 1953.

Barfield, Owen. *Poetic Diction: A Study in Meaning.* 3rd ed. Middletown, Conn.: Wesleyan University Press, 1973.

————. *The Rediscovery of Meaning and Other Essays.* Middletown, Conn.: Wesleyan University Press, 1977.

Bate, Walter Jackson. *Criticism: The Major Texts.* New York: Harcourt Brace Jovanovich, 1970.

Bosworth, Joseph. *An Anglo-Saxon Dictionary.* Ed. and enl. T. Northcote Toller. Oxford: Clarendon Press, 1898.

Carpenter, Humphrey. *Tolkien: A Biography.* Boston: Houghton Mifflin, 1977.

————. *The Inklings: C.S. Lewis, J.R.R. Tolkien, Charles Williams, and their Friends.* Boston: Houghton Mifflin, 1979.

Cassirer, Ernst. *Myth and Language.* Trans. Susanne K. Langer. New York: Harper and Brothers, 1946; rpt. New York: Dover Publications, 1953.

Hall, John R. Clark. *A Concise Anglo-Saxon Dictionary.* 3rd ed., rev. and enl. Cambridge: Cambridge University Press, 1931.

Helms, Randel. *Tolkien and the Silmarils.* n.p.: Houghton Mifflin, 1981.

Lewis, C.S., ed. *Essays Presented to Charles Williams.* London: Oxford University Press, 1947.

Nitzsche, Jane Chance. *Tolkien's Art: A "Mythology for England."* London: MacMillan Press, 1979.

Noel, Ruth S. *The Languages of Tolkien's Middle-earth.* Boston: Houghton Mifflin, 1980.

Pokorny, Julius. *Indogermanisches Etymologisches Wörterbuch.* Bern: Francke Verlag, 1959-.

Salu, Mary, and Robert T. Farrell, eds. *J.R.R. Tolkien: Scholar and Storyteller—Essays in Memoriam.* Ithaca: Cornell University Press, 1979.

Sugerman, Shirley, ed. *Evolution of Consciousness: Studies in Polarity.* Middletown, Conn.: Wesleyan University Press, 1977.

Tolkien, J.R.R. *"Beowulf:* The Monsters and the Critics," from *Proceedings of the British Academy,* XXII. London: Oxford University Press, 1937. Reprinted in *An Anthology of Beowulf Criticism,* ed. Lewis E. Nicholson. South Bend, Ind.: University of Notre Dame Press, 1963.

————. "Chaucer as a Philologist: *The Reeve's Tale*," *Transactions of the Philological Society*. London: David Nutt, 1934.

————. *The Letters of J.R.R. Tolkien*. Ed. Humphrey Carpenter with Christopher Tolkien. Boston: Houghton Mifflin, 1981.

————. *The Lord of the Rings*. 3 vols. New York: Ballantine Books, 1965.

————. *The Road Goes Ever On: A Song Cycle*. Poems by J.R.R. Tolkien set to music by Donald Swann. Boston: Houghton Mifflin, 1967.

————. *The Tolkien Reader*. New York: Ballantine Books, 1966; rpt. 1979.

————. *Unfinished Tales of Númenor and Middle-earth*. Ed. Christopher Tolkien. Boston: Houghton Mifflin, 1980.

SUGGESTED READING

Below is a list of readings designed to supplement the Bibliography and lead the interested reader to a variety of things directly or indirectly connected to Tolkien's thought and work.

Barfield, Owen. *Romanticism Comes of Age*. Letchworth: Rudolf Steiner Press, 1966.

————. *Unancestral Voice*. Middletown, Conn.: Wesleyan University Press, 1965.

————. *What Coleridge Thought*. Middletown, Conn.: Wesleyan University Press, 1971.

————. *Worlds Apart*. Middletown, Conn.: Wesleyan University Press, 1963.

Jaynes, Julian. *The Origin of Consciousness in the Breakdown of the Bicameral Mind*. Boston: Houghton Mifflin, 1976.

Jones, Roger S. *Physics as Metaphor*. Minneapolis: University of Minnesota Press, 1982.

Neumann, Erich. *The Origins and History of Consciousness*. Trans. R.F.C. Hull. Bollingen Series XLII. Princeton: Princeton University Press, 1970.

Shippey, T.A. *The Road to Middle-earth*. London: George Allen and Unwin, 1982.

Tolkien, J.R.R. *Finn and Hengist: The Fragment and the Episode*. Ed. Alan Bliss. London: George Allen and Unwin, 1982.

————. *The Monsters and the Critics and Other Essays*. Ed. Christopher Tolkien. London: George Allen and Unwin, 1983.

————. *The Old English Exodus*. Ed. Joan Turville-Petre. Oxford: Clarendon Press, 1981.

Wheeler, John Archibald. "The Universe as Home for Man." *American Scientist* 62 (Nov.-Dec., 1974): 683-691.

Whorf, Benjamin Lee. *Language, Thought, and Reality*. Ed. John B. Carroll. Cambridge, Mass.: M.I.T. Press, 1945.

INDEX